RADIANT

Middle-class recruits to C

Based on lectures and seminars held at
Gresham College March 2013 and May 2014

NICHOLAS DEAKIN
and
RODERICK FLOUD, KEVIN MORGAN,
GEOFF ANDREWS

JANE BERNAL, PHILIP COHEN, NORMA COHEN,
HAMISH MACGIBBON AND ELIZABETH DOLAN

Cover and book design by Julia Stubenboeck, out-of-habit.com

Published by Eden Valley Editions
1 Fircroft Way
Edenbridge
Kent TN8 6EL
www.eveeditions.com
Email: eve@topfoto.co.uk
+44 (0)1732 863939

EDEN VALLEY

EDITIONS

First published 2015
ISBN: 978-0-9929723-2-5
Printed and bound in the UK by Hato Press

When Adam delved and Eve span
Who was then the gentleman

CONTENTS

LIST OF ILLUSTRATIONS

PREFACE

NICHOLAS DEAKIN

This book is based on three seminars held at Gresham College, London, in March 2013 and May 2014.

In the introduction that follows this note, the then Provost of Gresham College, Sir Roderick Floud, explains how the exercise came about and why the organisers felt that the topic of middle-class recruits to communism in Britain during the 1930s deserved further attention.

I introduced the subject at the first seminar, and developed it in the second session. My essay in this volume is based on the two presentations I made in March 2013, lightly edited. As I explain, the material I drew upon for these sessions is based partly on discussion with the relatives of those who joined the Party during this period and their family papers.

At the second of the sessions in March 2013, further discussion of the topic was introduced by a panel consisting of Peter Hennessy, Juliet Gardiner and Denis Healey. Lord Healey's contribution was of particular interest, given that he was himself one of the few surviving members of the generation being discussed. We have therefore included later in the text a brief summary of his contribution, together with a note of some of the other points raised.

At the May 2014 seminar presentations were made by Professor Kevin Morgan, further exploring the general background to the recruitment of middle-class members to the CPGB, and by Geoff Andrews on James Klugmann, one of the outstanding members of this generation.

At the same session, there were contributions by several family members of recruits to the Party during this period. Five of these have been edited for inclusion in this volume: Jane Bernal discussing her mother, Margot Heinemann, Philip and Norma Cohen on their parents, Eve and Eric Cohen, and uncle, Len Jones, Hamish MacGibbon on his father, James, and Elizabeth Dolan on her parents Richard Clark and Mary McIntosh.

The final section of the book summarises some of the discussion that took place at this session, draws some provisional conclusions and suggests possible lines for further work on the subject.

The title of the book is drawn from the autobiography of one of the members of this generation, the poet C Day Lewis.

ACKNOWLEDGMENTS

First of all, thanks go to Gresham College for acting as hosts for the project and Valerie Shrimplin, the Academic Registrar and her colleagues for all the trouble they took to make the events there so successful. As is the practice with the College, the presentations at the three seminars are accessible on line through the College's website (www.gresham.ac.uk). The College has also made a transcript available of the points made during the very lively discussions that took place.

My colleagues on the project and I are grateful to all those who took part in the panel discussions and subsequent debates at Gresham College and especially to Denis Healey, Peter Hennessy and Juliet Gardiner, whose authoritative contributions helped to extend our understanding of the period.

Next, I would like to thank the editorial group for their support and in particular Ronnie McIntosh for his tireless energy and enthusiasm for the project from its conception onwards. Elizabeth Dolan has provided many insights as to how to improve this book, and Roderick Floud has given advice and support throughout this rather long process. I am also particularly grateful to Kevin Morgan for the thoughtful and considerate way in which he responded to my initial approach for help.

Much editorial work was required in order to transform the Gresham lectures and discussions into a book. Most of this was undertaken by Lucy Gaster. Anne Derges helped with the copy editing. On the design and production side, Julia Stubenboeck was mainly responsible, with the help of substantial advice and support from Fred Deakin. Lydia Syson and Nat Hunter also made significant contributions at various stages in the project. I am very grateful to all of them.

Nicholas Deakin, *September 2015*

INTRODUCTION

RODERICK FLOUD

The children of communists in the 1930s – many of whom have contributed to this book – experienced a very different world from that of their fathers and mothers. Most were still very young or even unborn in 1945. By that time, fascism had been defeated; as they grew up, the unemployment, hunger marches and poverty of the interwar years was to be replaced by full employment and the welfare state; the United Nations took the place of the League of Nations. But, at the same time, one of Britain's great allies in the battle against Nazism, the Soviet Union, had become its enemy in a Cold War that often threatened a nuclear holocaust; moreover, the terrible cruelties of Soviet communism, as well as its many inefficiencies as an economic system, became increasingly clear in the 1950s and thereafter.

Those children thus grew up at a time when many, if not all, of their parents found that their political allegiances, formed in the circumstances of the 1920s and 1930s, were severely tested. As the essays in this book demonstrate, for most of the older generation the decision to join or at least support the Communist Party in the 1930s (or, for a few, the 1920s) had stemmed from a revulsion against the consequences of the great depression and a conviction that only communism, in the shape of the Soviet Union, would stand up against the forces of fascism, whose evil was demonstrated in Spain, in Abyssinia and in Germany. Others joined because of admiration for what had been achieved in the aftermath of Tsarism, from an idealistic hope for the opportunities of a workers' state, or from a belief that they were witnessing the collapse of capitalism. They were not necessarily blind to the deficiencies of communism and the Soviet Union – the experiences of Orwell and others in Spain, news of the purges and, perhaps above all, the Nazi-Soviet pact opened many eyes – but they regarded the defeat of Hitler and Mussolini as the paramount objective of the late 1930s, an objective which other political forces in Britain – in particular the Conservative Party – came to share almost too late.

After 1945, however, many Communists and ex-Communists found that their motives and actions were increasingly viewed through a new prism, that of the anti-communism of the Cold War. Support for the Soviet Union, which had seemed natural and was indeed shared by the bulk of the population at the time of the siege of Stalingrad and the Russian convoys, was now increasingly portrayed as naïve, deluded or even treacherous. Careers of communists in the civil service, academia and other professions were never made impossible, but some found promotions blocked or felt themselves, to use Eric Hobsbawm's word, 'excluded.' Moreover, although Britain never descended into the hysterical depths of American McCarthyism, history was increasingly rewritten to paint those who had embraced communism in the 1930s as potential threats to Britain in the 1950s, 1960s and later decades, even if they had long ago renounced the political faith of their youth.

Inevitably, different men and women reacted in different ways to these changing circumstances. For some – though very few – there was no need to change; they retained their defiant faith in communism and their membership of the Communist Party until the end. Indeed, some of them outlived the Party itself. Some invested hope and energy in a non-Soviet version of communism. But most – some before the war but many during and after it – left the Party, some renouncing politics entirely, others moving to the Labour Party, some even further to the right. Successive crises, Yugoslavia in the 1940s, Hungary in the 1950s, the Berlin wall and Czechoslovakia in the 1960s, convinced them that they could no longer support the Party or the Soviet Union which lay behind it. For some, faith in Marxism as an intellectual framework survived disillusionment with its political advocates.

These decisions, as well as the original impulse to join communism in the 1930s, were not always easy to explain to their children or, perhaps, even to themselves. All of us are prone to rationalise our actions and all of us harbour residual regrets for some past decisions. But explaining those actions became much more difficult as the tides of anti-communism, the Cold War and successive 'spy scandals' swept across the countries of the western world. For some, those tides delayed decisions which, intellectually, they knew they should take; they did not wish to be disloyal to their comrades. Others took refuge in silence, refusing to discuss their past as communists or – as can so easily happen in families – made it clear that it was a subject that was not to be mentioned. Those who had been secret members of the Party faced particular conflicts.

All these factors mean that, both for individuals and for our society collectively, there are many gaps in our knowledge, and perhaps even more in our understanding, of the reasons why so many men and women, from all social groups, joined the communist movement and then, over later decades, largely left it. The purpose of this book is to attempt to fill those gaps, by pooling knowledge of the decisions of different people and identifying sources of information which can illuminate them. One such source is the records of MI5, which monitored the Communist Party throughout its existence; some, but by no means all, of those records have been released to the National Archives, though usually 'redacted' – allegedly to protect their sources.

The genesis of this book lies in a letter which I wrote to *The Times*. I complained that the security services would not allow me access to their file about my father, Bernard Floud, who was a communist in the 1930s and 1940s, a civil servant and later a Labour MP. He had been the subject, some 13 years after his death by suicide in 1967, of allegations by Chapman Pincher and others that he had been an 'agent of influence'; it emerged, with the publication of Peter Wright's *Spycatcher*, that my father had been interrogated by Wright in the months before his death, and that this was the source of Pincher's information (Wright, 1987). Subsequently, the allegations were considered by Professor Christopher Andrew in *The Defence of the Realm*: the authorised history of MI5, which concluded – presumably on the basis of my father's file – that, 'There was – and is – no evidence that he had any Communist contacts after 1952' when he left the Party (Andrew, 2009). Nor, apparently, is there any evidence that he supplied secret information to the Communist Party, although he certainly, in the 1930s, recruited others to its membership.

Despite the publication of Andrew's work, MI5 continues to refuse me access to the file until, possibly, 2017 – fifty years after my father's death. This is particularly annoying, and painful, since there is evidence from Andrew's book that the file is seriously inaccurate; in the first edition Andrew refers to the MI5 questioning of my father being suspended in January 1967 after 'Floud's wife, a former student Communist whom he had met at Oxford, committed suicide following a long period of mental illness'. This is totally untrue; my mother died in University College Hospital from collapsed lungs following a lifetime suffering from asthma. She had had bouts of agoraphobia but this did not contribute in any way to her death. I am grateful to Professor Andrew for removing this inaccuracy from the second edition of his book, but I am left with the question – which cannot be answered without access to the MI5 files – of what other inaccuracies are contained within them.

However, my letter to *The Times* produced one pleasant result; I was contacted by Sir Ronald McIntosh, a most distinguished civil servant who had worked with my father in the Board of Trade in the late 1940s. Ronnie told me of his admiration for my father and his conviction that he was an honourable man and said that he did not believe my father had been a Soviet spy (for more on this, see McIntosh, 2014). We met and, in the course of several conversations, agreed that there was far too little information available in the public domain about the reasons why so many – my father and mother and his sister and brother-in-law among them – had joined the Communist Party in the 1930s, and that this lack of knowledge had contributed to a skewing of the historical record. They were portrayed – with the hindsight of the Cold War – as mistaken, naïve or actively treacherous, rather than as young men and women convinced of the need to fight fascism by the most effective methods available to them. We also agreed that there was a special problem in the portrayal of young middle class communists as particularly deluded, or particularly hypocritical in 'rejecting their class'; it seems to be felt that, in some way, they should have known better.

Ronnie and I decided to pursue a variety of routes to try to redress this skewing and to produce, in the public domain, a balanced historical account. We were fortunate ultimately to enlist Professor Nicholas Deakin into the project and to be able to interest Gresham College, of which I was then Provost, in incorporating a lecture, a panel discussion and ultimately a seminar, into its programme. It is the edited version of these occasions which is the basis of this book. I, and Ronnie, are most grateful to Nicholas Deakin, to the contributors to this volume and to those who attended the Gresham events, as well as to Gresham College itself, for all the work and thought that has gone into its production.

CHAPTER ONE: THE RADIANT ILLUSION

NICHOLAS DEAKIN

INTRODUCTION

Until recently, young idealists from middle-class backgrounds who joined the CPGB in the 1930s have been too easily dismissed as 'Stalin's useful idiots', or as children of the bourgeoisie suffering from acute class guilt. At best, they are portrayed as blinkered and naïve, foolishly adopting positions that they didn't fully understand. At worst, they were faux durs, childishly playing at being tough-minded revolutionary cadres. At times, the dismissal has been brutal, as some observations after the death of Eric Hobsbawm demonstrated. In response, Karl Miller commented that:

'One of the most dismal prejudices to be encountered in Anglo-America has been its worsening failure to imagine how decent people could choose to be communists in the 1930s' (Miller, 2012)

Similarly, the decade in which they joined, the thirties, is habitually described in Auden's terms as low and dishonest, the 'devil's decade', a 'dark valley' leading inevitably to the armageddon in the second world war. The narrative arc leads inexorably downwards, leaving little space for laudable aspirations or even the positive achievements of that period – and they were considerable, as Juliet Gardiner has recently reminded us. (Gardiner, 2010)

However, many of the justifications for dismissing this generation and their experiences are essentially cold war arguments. Their choices were wrong because they are retrospectively invalidated by our knowledge about the truth of Stalin's dictatorship and the postwar history of Soviet Communism.

A fresh look now, twenty-odd years after the end of the cold war and the demise of both the Soviet Union and the CPGB, can take us beyond these stereotypes. But it is important to stress that this exercise is not intended as an apologia – it is simply an attempt at securing a better understanding of the motivation and attitudes of a group of young people, not a post-Soviet-style rehabilitation process.

SOME CONTEXT FOR THIS EXERCISE

The historian John Saville, himself one of the most interesting figures in the thirties generation, has commented that, 'analytical examples of the Communist experience are rare, in personal terms especially' (Saville, 2003: 8). Fortunately, through the diligence of Kevin Morgan and his Manchester colleagues, there is now quite a wide range of published accounts available (Morgan et al, 2007; McIlroy et al, 2001).

In addition, I had access for the purpose of preparing my lectures to a number of personal accounts and private papers of young middle-class people who decided to join the Communist Party during the 1930s. Discussion with family members (including my own) helped me to identify themes that would explain the various stages through which these young people passed - the trajectory that led to their decisions to join. These were the starting points for my exploration of public and private archives, written biographies and autobiographies and other literature, notably the CPGB archive material held at the People's History Library in Manchester. When drawing on these sources I have avoided emphasising well known celebrity cases; and I have tried not to engage with espionage, actual or imagined. Rather, I have used the individual experiences, some of which I refer to in the text, to help me to understand the motivations of those who joined the CPGB in this period and explore some of the consequences of their engagement with the Party.

As Roderick Floud points out in his introduction, there have been good reasons until the recent past why those with family connections with communism during the 1930s have felt inhibited from exploring this topic. The general willingness we found to participate in the present exercise, including the responses at three well attended seminars at Gresham College, was eloquent testimony in itself that the time has now come when these issues can be addressed without the burden of past prejudices.

THE THIRTIES BACKGROUND

All those who were young adults during the thirties had in common certain formative experiences that touched their whole generation. In particular, there was the first world war – the Great War to contemporaries. This cast a heavy shadow over the following decades, even in the victor nations. In one of them, Britain, the material sacrifices made to secure victory left a substantial impact on the national economy; but the human cost of the war in terms of deaths and injuries was perhaps the most important legacy. The young men and women of the early thirties did not themselves experience war directly, but their fathers, uncles and often their elder brothers had done so, and many of them had died or been permanently affected, physically or mentally. Other consequences were less immediate but equally significant – the war widows left to bring up children alone, and the other young women who would never find a partner.

Postwar Britain became a country in which the cult of mourning was all-pervasive, from the plaques in school halls, through the village memorials, regimental banners laid up in cathedrals to the Cenotaph in Whitehall: all forming part of the commemorations on Armistice Day, the focus both for grief but also of a rejection of militarism and its consequences. The lessons taught by the war poets, particularly Wilfred Owen, on the futility of war, were reinforced by the runaway success at the end of the twenties of R.C. Sherriff's play, *Journey's End*, which caught a national mood with its poignant account of ordeal, sacrifice and pervasive sense of loss. The determination that there would be no repetition of the slaughter in the trenches ran through all social classes, from the monarch downwards. At the time of the Abyssinian crisis in 1935, George V told his former Prime Minister Lloyd George that he would 'go to Trafalgar Square and wave a Red Flag myself' in protest if there were any question of war (Brendon, 2000: 354).

More practical ways of avoiding a resumption of war in Europe and beyond were based on the machinery created as part of the postwar settlement, most conspicuously the League of Nations, but also a major sequence of diplomatic negotiations designed to secure treaty commitments to significant reductions in the amounts of armaments held by major powers.

The economic depression that swept across the world at the end of the twenties proved fatal to these hopes. In Germany the impact of the depression fatally undermined the fragile Weimar Republic and opened the door to Hitler and his demagogic, anti-semitic National Socialism. Hitler was committed to reversing the Versailles settlement, and he made his intentions abundantly clear in mass demonstrations and on the streets.

The League of Nations was confronted with a series of progressively stronger challenges to its authority, beginning with Japan's invasion of Manchuria in 1931 - and failed all of them. Negotiations on reduction of armaments faltered in the face of the new realpolitik.

The economic effects in Britain of the depression were also substantial and the political outcome was dramatic. The second Labour Government fell in 1931 and was replaced by an all-party National Government. That government then won a general election in which the Labour Party lost almost all its leading figures and proceeded to introduce a programme of drastic cuts in public expenditure.

The social and economic consequences of the crisis were felt unevenly across the country and between classes. Many middle-class households were shielded to a considerable extent during the thirties from the full impact of the depression, being protected by the stability of much white-collar employment and the rapid expansion during the thirties of house ownership. Their experience contrasted sharply with that of the working classes outside London and the South-East. The collapse of manufacturing industry across South Wales, the Midlands, the North East and central Scotland resulted in endemic unemployment and acute poverty, with a crisis in public health. The extent of accessible relief was limited and still further restricted when cuts in government expenditure on social welfare led to the introduction in 1931 of the much-hated Means Test. (Gardiner 2010: 47-51)

The middle-class young, separately educated and living in single class suburbs or rural communities with their traditional hierarchies saw all this human misery at one remove, if at all. Though the more prosperous still had servants, there was generally a limited amount of personal contact across classes. This division was acutely felt by young idealists; as one of them, Christopher Mayhew, subsequently put it:

'I had no understanding of working class people. Millions of victims of capitalist oppression did exist, for sure, but I did not know any of them; or at least I did not know any of them well enough to understand how they felt. The working class was an abstraction, a trump card in political debate.'
(Mayhew 1982: 18)

Their experience was quite unlike that of their fathers and older brothers, who had lived alongside their fellow countrymen in the trenches and were often marked for life by that experience. Nevertheless some awareness of the realities of life outside the Home Counties, and the impact of mass unemployment did penetrate, becoming increasingly visible through demonstrations involving the unemployed, protesting vigorously about lack of work and the injustices of the Means Test. An inchoate sense developed that 'something needed to be done'. Where should the young turn for an answer?

The initial responses of the small group whose experiences I have explored – anxiety, concern, desire to do things better – were similar to those of many of their contemporaries.

But where they were not typical was in the choice that they made: to join the Communist Party. They did so despite the fact that, contrary to some later accounts, there were other choices open to them.

What was it that led them in this particular direction? Was there something distinctive about their personalities? The character and beliefs of their parents? Their own intellectual curiosity? Their class situation or even ethnic origins?

Or was their choice determined by circumstances – opportunities and restrictions in the educational institutions they attended, individual encounters and friendships, interests and cast of mind, even their sexual relationships? And what do their stories have to tell us about the particular appeal of communism to this generation?

In tracing their experiences and that of their contemporaries I have framed my narrative – which will necessarily be much condensed – in terms of life cycle, from family background through education and wider experiences in adolescence and after, through the decision to join the Party and its immediate consequences.

The proposition that a propensity to join 'radical organisations' can be explained by the presence of pathological personality disorders was a typical product of the cold war literature. As far as Britain is concerned this theory was conclusively rebutted by Kenneth Newton's pioneering study of British communism (Newton 1969). This theme was revisited by Jenifer Hart in her frank autobiography (Hart 1998), in which she convincingly dismisses any such explanation of her own decision to join the Party.

There are slightly more plausible explanations on offer around the dynamics of the family, specifically relations with the dominant parent – usually, though not invariably, the father. The older generation's unwillingness to understand, let alone sympathise with the younger generation's aspirations is of course a constant theme in most post enlightenment societies and provided the motif for many a bildungsroman. In his preface to the biography of Donald Maclean, Noel Annan makes pretentious reference to the Priesthood of Nemi, where each priestly generation is in turn symbolically slain by its successor. (Cecil 1988: xi) Kingsley Amis is more forthright – his communism was simply a 'banal' rebellion against his father. (Leader 2006: 109) However, in the small group I've followed, good – if not always close and affectionate – relationships with parents is the common pattern – parents who often have 'liberal' views themselves and are anxious to understand what is driving their children further to the left.

So in these cases, at least, the decision to commit to communism needs further explanation; possibly in the search for a credible faith, another feature of many adolescences, which could take conventional religious form but might then be diverted into new channels when that religion came to seem inadequate or even oppressive.

But to explain the decision made by young middle class idealists, the education system is the logical next place in which to look. For them this usually, but by no means invariably, meant public schools (progressive schools, especially for girls, provided a slightly different environment).

YOUNG RADICALS AT SCHOOL

Rebellion against the institutions and values of public schools, as they were in the nineteen twenties, hardly needs special explanation. But one cause that attracted widespread symbolic opposition and engaged the pacifist instincts of many of the young was the requirement to undertake military training in the Officer Training Corps. Individuals took this cause up and there were some efforts to extend support for rejection across schools, as through Esmond Romilly's publication *Out of Bounds*. Individual radical teachers were also an influence in a number of schools.

But systematic attempts by pupils at working up alternative approaches, rather than simply another version of youthful nay-saying or small 'cells' of self-proclaimed communists, seem to have been quite rare, compared with what was happening in continental Europe in lycées and gymnasia.

The most spectacular exception that I have found was Westminster School. This school was unusual at the time (and indeed subsequently) in the extent to which students there were open to the outside world, being located in the centre of London and with direct links into the world of politics. It was a standard feature of a pupil's experience there to be addressed at school societies by leading politicians, whose views were often subjected to critical examination and debate. A lively culture of discussion – including a very active League of Nations youth group – existed within the school.

Figure 1 **Westminster School.** Westminster pupils outside Ashburnham House in Little Dean's Yard in the 1930s. (Reproduced by kind assistance of the Governing Body of Westminster School)

Against this background, it is less surprising that in 1936 a group of students in the scholars' house, with the encouragement of a number of teachers, should have sought and obtained permission to establish a political society with the explicit aim of producing a manifesto on current world issues to which the adherence of fellow pupils would be sought. This was to be reinforced by a programme of regular meetings and publications explaining the different items in the manifesto. This group was called (with the headmaster's grudging consent) the United Front of Popular Forces ('Uffpuff'). The group managed a year's lively existence and then, as these things do, faded away, leaving behind impressive evidence of the seriousness of the attempts made to communicate advanced political ideas and secure commitment to them.

Westminster pupils were also able to use their freedom to move about London to attend the political demonstrations that were becoming an increasingly common feature of the capital. School magazines report attendance at a number of rallies, for example, a big CPGB meeting in Trafalgar Square and the 1936 May Day rally addressed by the Party's leader Harry Pollitt (described as 'most stirring and extremely lucid'). Jack Gaster, a recent convert to the Communist Party from the ILP, spoke at the first and 'won the sympathy of the crowd with a few well-chosen wisecracks at the expense of the National Government' (School Archive).

The students were sufficiently impressed by these experiences to attempt to invite Harry Pollitt to speak at the school, but liberalism could not stretch that far (although Uffpuff sent their manifesto to him and received an encouraging response).

Other schools also had distinctive qualities that helped to shape the views of their would-be radical pupils. The biographer of the Communist poet, Randall Swingler, described him as a high caste Wykehamist in flight from his education and class but retaining that school's sense of public service. (Croft 2001) Swingler is not the only Wykehamist I have

Figure 2 **Harry Pollitt.** During the thirties Harry Pollitt, the CPGB's **General Secretary,** was the public face of the Party, his oratory much admired even **by his opponents.** Here, he is addressing members of the International Brigade, in Spain (September 1937). (Photo: People's History Museum, Manchester.)

encountered – Charles Madge is described by his then wife, Kathleen Raine, as being the centre of a coterie of left-wing Wykehamists. (Raine 1975: 80) Another of the same tribe was Thomas Hodgkin, whose entertaining verse autobiography *Don Tomas* (alas, cut off by his death before completion) lovingly lists his school contemporaries (Swingler among them) and their congenial views. Frank Thompson, platonic lover of Iris Murdoch, who recruited him into the Party, also saw himself as a member of an elite, although he thought that 'the culture one imbibed at Winchester was too nostalgic ... one fell in love with the beauty of the past'. This despite the left wing teacher who hung up a map of the Spanish civil war in the classroom and taught 'Russian, German and current affairs' (Conradi 2012:86).

Other schools stand out as having a culture which was sympathetic to more radical views. Gresham's, the school attended by W.H.Auden, Bernard Floud and his brother Peter and James Klugmann (Andrews 2015), was a place that formally rejected jingo patriotism and was prepared to tolerate reformist, even socialist ideas.

Girls' day schools in London were also an environment in which radical views could be shared and openly expressed. Their pupils were, as Jenifer Hart puts it, 'often already thoughtful, not uncomprehending of the issues of the day' (Hart 1998: 63) and frequently developed a strong interest in public affairs, as Maire Lynd and Margot Heinemann did. (Bernal, loc cit). Some of them were subsequently anxious to rebut the patronising suggestion that they were recruited into the Party not of their own volition but merely by following their boyfriends.

Meanwhile, there were other ways of learning about political developments abroad, through formal links between public schools in England and those in continental Europe or informally through trips to Germany, in particular holidays with parents and friends or to learn the language.

The most spectacular of these possibilities was a trip to the USSR. To take a Westminster example again, the school magazine (December 1932) contains an account of David Hubback's trip on the Soviet ship Kooperatia. His verdict was cautiously favourable: '… a land of hope, if not yet of glory' (School Archive).

The specific fascination with the USSR blended with a more general russophilia – and in particular a taste for Russian literature. This could be reinforced by attendance at the White Russian exile Prince Dmitri Mirsky's London University courses. In 1929 the Prince defected to Marxism and began to deploy a very different sort of analytical approach (Smith 2012). One of those who attended his subsequent lectures was François Lafitte, who was also involved directly, while in Germany before going up to Oxford in 1932, in active resistance to Nazism in the street, as Eric Hobsbawm was, more dramatically (Hobsbawm 2002: 71-73).

Other radical schoolboys found an outlet in expressing support for the Bulgarian communist Dimitrov at the Reichstag Fire trial or in concern about the suppression of the Social Democrats in Vienna and clandestine activity taken to help them out (as described in an article in the Westminster School magazine strikingly entitled 'Austro-Marxismus').

There was another avenue for conversion: simple intellectual curiosity, leading to an individual's own choice to read the Marxist classics and reflect upon them.

But in most cases the moment of choice came in higher education, which for this group meant Oxford, Cambridge or possibly the London School of Economics. However, as Donald Maclean's biographer comments, 'It is easy to overlook how many undergraduates reached university ripe for recruitment' (to the CP) (Cecil 1988:16), and also the strength of feeling associated with their experiences at school. Commenting in the mid-thirties on this strong reaction against their public schools, the Oxford student magazine *Isis* observed:

'It is in the interests of Conservatism that the public schools be destroyed before they turn loose too many bitter young Socialists and Communists. If the latter wish to make the country a Communist state, they really should insist that everyone is sent to a public school.' (Mayhew 1987:24)

UNIVERSITY OPTIONS

From 1933 onwards, new undergraduates who came up to the two oldest English universities or LSE and wished to take some part in radical activities would find a whole range of possibilities.

Not all of those attracted to progressive politics were the children of established middle class intelligentsia – most often referred to as the 'gilded youth'– some were the first generation of their family in higher education. As Harry Ferns comments in his autobiography about those who joined the Party during his time at Cambridge:

'All the people of high intelligence in Cambridge did not become Communists. Far from it. But those who did were nearly all people of high intelligence measured in terms of academic achievement. They were not all public school boys and the female equivalent. Some came from humble homes and some from upper-middle-class and aristocratic background ... Schooling and social background do not explain membership in the Communist Party in Cambridge at that time.' (Ferns 1983: 117)

At Cambridge, the student left were united in a single grouping, the Cambridge University Socialist Club, with a core communist group, of which David Haden Guest was principal mover (Kiernan et al 2003: 39-59). They worked under the patronage of a small number of dons, as members of the Party cell whose origins can be traced to a meeting in 1931 of the Heretics Club addressed by Comrade-Prince Dmitri Mirsky. Frances Cornford, reporting to her son John who could not be there, described him as believing in Communism 'like a Byzantine saint, with a wonderful smile' (Smith 2012: 207). In Oxford (where most of the people I am discussing went) there was a wider range of possibilities in the early thirties.

First, the October Club, founded in 1931 by an American student, Frank Meyer and his friend Dick Freeman – effectively the nucleus of the communist presence – though there had been a few individual members earlier. The decision by Meyer and Freeman to take their small group formally into the Party was triggered off by a visit to the Club by the briefly ubiquitous Mirsky (now unequivocally Comrade).

Second, a University Labour Club, shortly to be revived by a Canadian, David Lewis, after going into sharp decline after the traumatic fall of the Labour Government in 1931. A vigorous student Liberal grouping; a strong League of Nations Union and associated peace groupings, intent on promoting the Peace Ballot and the Peace Pledge Union.

Or on the other side, there were the fascists, initially quite strong in the University – cultivated by Mosley personally and by his movement – first as the New Party and subsequently as the British Union of Fascists.

And outside the explicitly political arena but a very active contender for the recruitment of the unattached, was the evangelical Christian 'Oxford Group' launched by Frank Buchman, modelling itself partly on twentieth century ideas about organised political action: propaganda, cells of believers, testimony of the converted. As its name implies, his movement was explicitly designed to appeal to university students as the potential leaders of tomorrow.

In the early thirties, the story is partly of uneasy relations between the Labour Club and other left wing groupings, but in December 1935 the club decided to sanction joint action with the October Club and the way was now formally open to collaboration with the communists. Simultaneous open membership of both the Communist and Labour parties was now possible, although the communists often preferred

Figure 3 **October Club.** Demonstration in 1934 calling for the release of the Chairman of the German Communist Party (KPD), Ernest Thalmann, who had been arrested when the Nazis came to power. Subsequently, the Bulgarian Communist, Georgi Dimitrov, had been tried and acquitted at the Reichstag Fire trial. The banner of the Oxford University October Club is prominently displayed. (Photo: Edith Tudor-Hart. National Galleries of Scotland)

to leave membership of their party undeclared. To grasp the full implications of this development we need to understand the nature of the CPGB at this time.

THE CPGB IN THE THIRTIES.

At the beginning of the 1930s the Communist Party (properly the Communist Party of Great Britain: British section of the Communist International) had been very small indeed, with around 2,500 members and locked into a fierce struggle to establish itself as the authentic party of the British working class, in opposition to the Labour Party and the existing trades union movement. This involved denunciations of the Labour Party as complicit in capitalist oppression of the workers and an attempt to create rival unions in key industries: the 'Minority Movement'. The form of the struggle and the objective – an attempt to create a British form of Bolshevism – was dictated by the line taken by the Comintern, based in Moscow and requiring implementation by national member parties. This policy was known as 'class against class' (Thompson 1992: 44ff).

The link with Moscow was explicit and it was both an asset and a handicap. It enabled the Party to bask in the reflected glory of a connection with the great Soviet experiment – 'actually existing socialism' – but it allowed its critics to write off the Party as an agent of a foreign power, obedient to a line set abroad and operating with the aid of Red Gold.

The Party at this stage was a classic Marxist-Leninist vanguard party of the industrial working class, the cadres formed in struggle and often trained at the Lenin School in Moscow. The Party was essentially factory-based and no attempt had been made to extend the class base of the membership; although a few middle-class members did join at this period, most did not remain.

This situation changed. The coming to power of the Nazis in 1933 clearly demonstrated the folly of the division between Social Democrats and Communists that had allowed them to do so. The Reichstag fire trial in the following year, with the Bulgarian Communist Georgi Dimitrov's epic defiance of the Nazi regime from the dock, and the suppression of the Austrian Social Democrats in Vienna underlined the urgency of organising effective resistance to the dictatorships. The Italian invasion of Abyssinia exposed the inability of the League of Nations to implement even the modest sanctions that had been agreed as an attempt to deter Mussolini's aggression. The USSR came in from the international cold by joining the League of Nations in 1934 (and Nazi Germany left). And the Comintern decreed the end of the 'class against class' policy (1935), now instructing member parties instead to form alliances of all left wing parties against Fascism.

In the USSR itself, the apparent success of the Five Year Plans was attracting a series of foreign visitors, most of them eager to be convinced that Soviet planning had the answer to the problems of unemployment and industrial modernisation which capitalism had failed to provide.

The extent of communist engagement in successive political developments in Britain grew: Oswald Mosley's campaigns after he shed his respectable supporters and embraced anti-semitism – notoriously, at his Olympia rally in 1934 – provided the battleground for his left-wing opponents. More positively, unemployment and hunger marches organised by the National Unemployed Workers Movement (NUWM) – a membership body led by the communist Wal Hannington – helped to dramatise the extent of unemployment, which had reached three million by 1934, and the conditions of life on the dole and the impact on public health.

And the Communist Party itself, released from the constraints of the 'class against class' policy, began the process of building alliances on

Figure 4 **Hunger March.** Marches organised by the National Unemployed Workers'
Movement were a very effective way of getting the Party's message across. (Photo:
People's History Museum, Manchester)

the left by opening negotiations with the Independent Labour Party (ILP), until recently reviled as 'social fascists' – though the Labour Party, unimpressed by the change of line, declined to engage in these discussions.

So the CPGB now positively welcomed the prospect of recruiting young middle class members. As Willie Gallacher, shortly to become the Party's only MP, put it when addressing undergraduates in Cambridge in 1934:

'We want people who are capable, who are good scientists, historians and teachers. It doesn't follow at all that you will be good workers. We need you as you are: if you have a vocation it is pointless to run away to factories. One or two of you may become full-time revolutionaries but this is a thing that only a few of you will be able to do. We want you to study and become good students.' (Clark et al 1979:32)

THE LEFT IN OXFORD

The range of activity expected of Oxford University Labour Club members, as demonstrated in the Club's bulletins from the mid-1930s, now broadens and deepens.

These involve first of all anti-war activities. The once notorious Oxford Union's 'King and Country' resolution of 1933 was a one-off without the wider implications later attributed to it. But action becomes more urgent after 1935 and the demonstrable failure of the League of Nations to find a means of dealing with Italy's military aggression in Abyssinia. This is the point at which the once-famous Peace Ballot was launched, which invited respondents to declare their views on the League, on reduction of armaments and national air forces by consent, and about the response to aggressors – either economic sanctions or in the last resort military measures. On all but the last item there were thumping majorities for the anti-war view. On the back of this the charismatic clergyman, Dick Sheppard, launched his Peace Pledge Union (PPU), in which individuals were invited to send pledge cards with the words: 'I renounce war and never again, directly, or indirectly, will I support or sanction another.' Membership nationally reached six figures by the end of 1936 (Ceadel 2010: 334 ff).

Next, there was the response to the hunger marches. The impact of their arrival in both universities was immediate and substantial: they provided visible evidence of the consequences of government policies towards the 'distressed areas' and, for some, the human contact previously lacking (Bernal loc cit). This leads on to the search for practical means of support for the unemployed, such as joint summer camps, involving student volunteers with Welsh miners (Hart 1998).

There was also joint working with the labour movement in Oxford City. Examples were the successful strike at the Pressed Steel factory (masterminded by Abe 'Firestone' Lazarus); and the attempt in 1935 to tear down the 'Cutteslowe Walls' dividing local authority from privately-owned housing (Collison 1963) .This linked to anti-fascist action – repelling Mosley's attempts to secure a base for his movement in Oxford (achieved in practice by 1936), assisting in confrontations elsewhere, and the development of Popular Front activities, stimulated by the electoral successes of the French Front Populaire and the Popular Front in Spain.

In all this, John Cornford, as a communist student organiser, played an important role (Sloan (ed) 1938; Stansky and Abrahams 1966). He inherited from Frank Meyer, who had mentored him before being deported in 1934, the task of making cross-university links, achieving a union between the communist-led Federation of Student Societies (FSS) and the University Labour Federation (ULF), and so providing a common platform for student campaigns.

But one particular cause now comes to dominate.

The military revolt against the Spanish Republic in 1936 marks a turning point in more ways than one. The involvement on the side of the rebels of Nazi Germany and Fascist Italy, whose military and logistic support was indispensable to their early successes, was only partly counterbalanced by the engagement of the USSR on the side of the Republic (Preston 2006).

The Comintern's decision to create an International Brigade (IB) of foreign volunteers offered a route to direct involvement in the struggle. In Britain, the Communist Party took the lead in organising recruitment and passage of recruits through France to the fighting. The first contingents of the Brigade arrived in Madrid in time to take part in the defence of the capital against Franco's assault and the successful resistance around the city's university which gave birth to the slogan: 'No pasaran!'

Meanwhile, the democracies, including the Popular Front government recently elected in France, committed themselves to a policy of non-intervention which purported (but failed) to limit the supplies of military equipment and 'volunteers' to both sides. In this policy, the National Government in Britain initially had the support of the Labour Party. From the perspective of the young, battle lines now appeared to be clearly drawn – fascism should and could be stopped and the place to do so was Spain. The issue was clearly summed up in the Spanish Republic's appeal for outside help: today us, tomorrow, you. Communists were already prominent on the Republican side in the defence of Madrid and subsequently formed the overwhelming majority of recruits from Britain to the International Brigade.

The alternative of collective security through the League of Nations — or of joint action by the democracies — now appeared to be incapable of providing an effective response to aggression. The non-

Figure 5 **Abe Lazarus,** sometimes known as 'Bill Firestone', was a Communist organiser in Oxford. (Photo by permission of Graham Stevenson)

Figure 6 **Pressed Steel Strike.** One of Lazarus' campaigns was to unionise the new Pressed Steel factory in Cowley. (Photo: the authors)

Figure 7 **Cutteslowe Walls.** Another campaign was to pull down the Cutteslowe Walls, built to divide a local Council estate from a private development. (Photo: Oxford Times)

intervention policy was a farce, allowing the rebels ready access to help from their allies, the right wing dictatorships, but blocking assistance to the legitimate government.

Events in Spain also presented a crisis for pacifists: there were many defections of socialist pacifists who now regarded the suppression of Franco's rebellion as a uniquely just cause for which it was right to fight.

Generally, the appeal of communism was greatly enhanced. As the International Brigades were drawn into a series of desperate confrontations with Franco's regular troops and his Italian allies, the list of the martyred dead grew rapidly longer. Prominent among them were some of the high profile middle-class recruits to the Party. And a whole series of ancillary activities in support of the Republic, beginning with Medical Aid for Spain, were eagerly promoted.

Of course the situation in Spain was not quite as clear-cut as contemporaries believed. But the image of Spain, the good cause to which all should commit themselves without reservation, dominated much debate on the left over the rest of the decade. Writers and poets in particular felt called upon to make their contribution. As one of them (Louis MacNeice) put it in his *Autumn Journal*: 'In Spain our blunt ideals would find their whetstone.'

CHOOSING COMMUNISM

All these developments now seemed to provide clear answers to the question: from all the options on offer, why choose communism?

Spain was the strongest card in the pack for those seeking to recruit newcomers to communism. But there were others.

The decision could take the form of a spontaneous 'crossing over' experience, instant or overnight. This is often compared to religious

Figure 8 **Spain shop.** As part of their campaign at home against the non-intervention policy, the CPGB collected material support for the Republic, as in this 'Spain' shop in Southwark (1937). (Photo: Edith Tudor-Hart, National Galleries of Scotland).

conversion, though others reject this parallel.[1] Rather, it might be a matter-of-fact conclusion, based on consideration of the evidence, reading and reflecting either over time or in a single moment, when everything that was previously confusing now fell into one logical and consistent pattern.

Or it might stem from considering the alternatives and finding them unsatisfactory. The failure of the capitalist system and the need for fundamental change and replacement by a new economic and social order was accepted across a wide spectrum of opinion. The Labour Party was frequently seen as being incapable of achieving the radical changes that would be required.

In choosing an alternative, there was a perception of the CPGB as the wave of the future and of individual communists as serious people, tough, committed, well informed, and able to get things done.

For 'outsiders' in social class or ethnic terms joining the Party could seem attractive as a means of moving towards acceptance in wider society, though this may have been particularly true for Jewish and Irish working-class members.

For feminist recruits, the Party might be seen as a means of addressing the frustrations of young middle-class women up against institutional discrimination in traditional professions (medicine, teaching, the civil service). Another factor might be the influence of lovers (especially working-class partners, heterosexual and gay).

Or it was a mixture of all these reasons, along with the eternal impulse of the young to throw the mighty down and smash the existing system: as one of them subsequently put it, the objective was that 'inequality, injustice, imperialism and war were all to be abolished' (Mayhew 1987: 18).

---

1 This argument is put forward by Raphael Samuel in *The Lost World of British Communism* (Verso 2006) esp p.67, with his own family as an example; but the wider application is doubted by Saville (p. 9).

And it could be the outcome of courtship by Party branches and their 'fishermen' in universities and professional groupings. Philip Toynbee gives a vivid account of that process in his memoir Friends Apart. (Toynbee 1954: 62) Gaster family papers show such courtships at work in exchanges between Maire Lynd and Michael Abercrombie. In his letters, he coaxes her gently towards closer involvement in Party activities – only about three hours per week but useful training and 'constructed for intellectuals' – supervises her reading and urges her to apply for membership as soon as she feels herself to be 'a convinced communist'. When she does, he turns her over to François Lafitte, the senior Party organiser, with a word of caution about not being put off by his manner.

Finally, there could be the shock of an individual event – the arrival of hunger marchers, an encounter with a working-class Party activist, a death in Spain – that clinched the decision to 'come over'.

And the Party itself was willing to welcome new recruits from a wide range of backgrounds; Harry Pollitt, speaking in 1937 at the Albert Hall, assured his audience that

'We have no contemptuous attitude towards the middle class and the professional people. We believe that unless we can win them to the side of the working class both they and ourselves will pay the same price as has already been paid in Germany, in Austria and in Italy.' (Pollitt 1937)

The Central Committee's report to the Party's Fourteenth Congress in the same year referred to the rapid increase in Party numbers and commented hopefully that,

'Many students and people connected with the professions have joined us, believing that only through the advancement of the aims of the Communist Party can they help towards the development of the new Socialist society.' (CPGB 1937)

Spain continued to be a main focus for student activity – not just campaigning to change Government policy on non-intervention, but medical aid and eventually helping refugees (like Basque children, cared for by young dons' wives).

Political action now stressed the importance of a Popular Front: after Munich, there was a practical example in the 1938 Oxford Parliamentary by-election in the (not entirely voluntary) withdrawal of the Labour candidate in favour of an independent progressive, the Master of Balliol, Alexander ('Sandy') Lindsay. There was heavy student engagement with his campaign (Healey 1990: 37).

Other favoured activities for progressive undergraduates included visits to the USSR (Mayhew 1987: 24). Trips with Intourist were an increasingly common experience for young enthusiasts (VOKS – All-Union Society for Cultural Relations with Foreign Countries – for grander visitors). Not all these journeys had happy outcomes from the hosts' point of view: there was scepticism about political motivation and revulsion at the catering and sanitary arrangements in the workers' state. But among those who went there was also some willingness to regard these as the teething problems of a new society and celebrate its achievements, both practical, like the White Sea Canal (actually built by slave labour), and philosophical, like the introduction of the 1936 Soviet Constitution (never actually implemented).

There was also an emphasis in the Party on exploring ways to expose exploitation in the Empire, and more particularly in India, involving recruitment of Indian and Ceylonese students as Party members (Ferns 1983: 90). In addition, there was work with the increasing numbers of refugees from Nazi Germany and eventually also Austria and Czechoslovakia.

For those coming up after 1936 there was, for some, a sense of impending doom – the Rhineland, Spain, Munich – a 'drum beat of war'? But this feeling does not seem to have been universal.

It is also important not to overemphasise the political dimension – this may have been all-absorbing for many, but by no means for all. Yet membership of the Oxford University Labour Club (OULC) by 1938 was impressive – one fifth of all students belonged. And CPGB student members were encouraged to set to work penetrating other organisations. Communists as office holders in the OULC were semi-legitimate; but positions were sought out in other bodies too, especially anti-war groups, like the League of Nations youth movement.[2]

And then there was the academic dimension. Denis Healey subsequently commented that whereas previously any communists at university '... were very sectarian, got drunk, wore beards and did not worry about examinations ....' now, especially after the introduction of the Popular Front policy, 'Communists started shaving, tried to avoid being drunk in public, worked for first class degrees and played down their Marxist-Leninism' (Healey 1990: 38). But not necessarily. Despite what Harry Ferns says, some Communists graduated with poor degrees, even a pass degree or no degree at all – two of these were to become professors. By the end of the thirties, there was much talk of 'fashionable and popular red Oxford'. epitomised by Frank Thompson (another Wykehamist) and the Iris Murdoch entourage. These communists were by no means swots, dullards or puritans. Rather, there seems to have been a standing invitation to theatricals – and the dance floor.

---

2   One example among many in the Lynd papers is a letter from an organiser of the League of Nations Youth 'fraction' asking for help.

Becoming a comrade meant joining a clerisy, a sacred band. As a condition of entry, the newcomer was committed to embarking on serious political (re)education, studying classic texts and learning how to apply Marxist principles. It meant taking on specific tasks as part of the Party's political work – meetings, canvassing, local campaigns, chalking, street corner public speaking and selling the *Daily Worker*.[3]

There were special assignments involving infiltration of existing organisations – youth and local branches of other political parties, peace organisations, professional bodies and trades union branches. It meant giving priority to the Party over the personal: entering a small world but also becoming part of an international movement centred on the USSR ('the socialist sixth of the world'), unconditional support for which was a fundamental principle of membership.

Negatively, it sometimes meant cutting off from friends and family who wouldn't tolerate the degree of commitment required. It also meant confronting the hostility of political opponents, including perhaps particularly, those elsewhere on the Left. In subsequent accounts George Orwell is frequently mentioned as an example; and there was increasingly frenetic hostility, mandated from Moscow, to 'Trotskyite deviations'. And it could also mean mockery – as in Cyril Connolly's squib *Where Engels fear to Tread*.

Comradeship in practice meant close identification with the working class and a fundamental change in attitudes and behaviour. This extends to name changes – more demotic first names, no more Ruperts, Evelyns, Gabriels or François. Sometimes there was an attempt to change accent, perhaps in the context of making practical links with the rapidly

---

3 For example, activities of middle-class recruits as described in Edward Upward's lightly fictionalised account in *In The Thirties* (Penguin 1969) or in Cecil Day Lewis *The Buried Day* (Chatto and Windus 1960)

growing Party presence in the Trades Unions, confirming that this is a party of the working class, to which middle class recruits now owed their primary loyalty.

It could also mean casual sexual relations 'within the Party' (Toynbee 1954: 61). The militant's own family could also become of secondary importance. The individual was 'of no importance', yet at the same time there were individual leaders who were of fundamental significance – Stalin, increasingly, as the thirties passed, Dimitrov as head of the Comintern, but also the CPGB's own leadership, especially Harry Pollitt.

Yet the CPGB differed in one important respect from almost all the other members of the Comintern. The Party was subject to frequent criticism and members often had to face much personal pressure. But before the outbreak of war, the Party never experienced the kind of active persecution that other Communist parties had to undergo. Individual communists were often accepted as potential allies, admired for their energy and willingness to take on uncongenial tasks, and able to lead a social and professional life that extended outside the Party's own world.

Some of this was reflected in the experiences of those who had either enlisted in the Party at university earlier in the decade or joined as a result of encounters in various professional settings, early in their working lives.

AFTERMATHS

Some of those who had committed themselves fully to communism initially saw their own future strictly in terms of Party work. This might involve being directly employed by the CPGB in organisational work with the membership of local branches under the direction of the regional Party apparatus.

For example, after going down in 1935 François Lafitte (now 'Frank') was a Party organiser in East London and in October 1936 it was his responsibility to communicate the London District Committee's decision not to oppose Mosley's march through the area but instead to concentrate on a youth rally for Spain in Trafalgar Square. The written instructions that he gave Joe Jacobs of the Stepney Party ('If Mosley attempts to march, let him. Don't attempt disorder') were swiftly overturned by the action taken by local activists and the District apparat accepted the inevitable.[4] The Battle of Cable Street then took place, and the image of unswerving communist resistance to fascism, so dear to the Party in later years, was born. (And François abandoned the work for which he himself believed he was entirely unsuited.)

Others became active members of local Party groups. For example, the Marylebone branch of the Party (to which Maire Lynd and Jack Gaster belonged) had a vigorous existence, campaigning for tenants' rights, seeking unsuccessfully to promote joint activities with the local Labour Party and raising funds for medical aid for Spain. We have a flickering portrait of their public activities from Special Branch surveillance reports which tell us that when the Branch celebrated their first five years 'songs of a communistic and satirical character' were sung (MI5 file (Gaster) 27.1.39) .

Others worked as student organizers – first nationally and then internationally (Klugmann; Floud) – helped build up anti-war groups (Madge) or worked with refugees. The League of Nations Union (LNU) proved to be fertile ground for penetration by young communists.

---

4   See Joe Jacobs *Out of the Ghetto* (Phoenix, 1991) pp. 241ff. 'Frank' Lafitte's written instructions are reproduced on pp 239/40

Figure 9 **Cable Street.** The local CP branch in Stepney was responsible for changing the Party's line and actively confronting Oswald Mosley's proposed march through East London. The resulting scenes show demonstrators in retreat from the police. (Photo: Jewish Chronicle)

Particular professional groups provided a sympathetic environment for the communist recruits, for example, the natural sciences. Many young scientists were persuaded by Soviet claims to have evolved, through 'scientific socialism', a means of rationally ordering society, and the apparent success of the Soviet Union in putting scientific discoveries to work for the common good, not profit, was very attractive. The lab frequently became a recruitment zone.[5]

The image of the Soviet Union as being in the vanguard of modernism and experiment in the arts and sciences was also potentially attractive. Soviet experiments in architecture were widely admired in that profession and in the then fashionable planning movement.

Engineering (the state's massive construction schemes), and aeronautics (the heroic deeds of Soviet aeronauts) were also the subject of much successful propaganda by the regime.

In the arts, there was admiration for the constructivists but particularly for Soviet cinema (especially documentaries recounting Soviet achievements, much shown at film clubs) and photography with a social purpose (Forbes 2013). Here, too, there was increased exposure to the eloquent and persuasive political émigrés from Europe.

As a result, an increasing number of artistic and cultural groups were set up – either based inside the Party or loosely connected to it – through which admiration for Soviet models and the application of modernist principles might serve to recruit new members or at least reinforce existing left-wing sympathies (MacGibbon loc cit).

At a more practical level, the widely remarked upon crisis in public health in the depression provided ample grounds for young medical

---

5 For example, Paul Broda's account of the recruitment of his step-father Alan Nunn May in *Scientist Spies* (Matador 2011) and his activities among scientific workers (p.55)

Figure 10 **Communist planning.** Local branches of the CPGB prepared ambitious plans for their localities - but in this case, the Party did not hold any seats on the local Borough Council. (Photo: the authors)

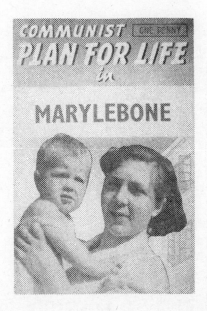

Figure 11 **A Party card.** Jack Gaster joined the CPGB from the ILP in 1936, and this is his first Party card. (Photo: the authors)

No..................

THE

COMMUNIST PARTY

OF GREAT BRITAIN

16, KING STREET
COVENT GARDEN
LONDON, W.C. 2.

This is to Certify that

Jack Gaster

of

is a Member of the Communist Party.

Marylebone Cell or Group

N. London Sub-District Local

Secretary

students to consider alternative approaches, and there was also the development of psychoanalysis as a profession, reinforced by the Hitler exiles.

In the social sciences there were pioneering social investigations, much enhanced by the contribution of exiles – Marie Jahoda, Ruth Durant, Robert Kuczynski – left wing though not open Party members. There was the creation of Mass Observation and Charles Madge's attempt to create a synthesis of his Marxism and Tom Harrisson's applied social anthropology (Madge 1986).

The creation of the Left Book Club in 1936 on the initiative of Victor Gollancz, provided a ready source of political information and analysis, intended to contribute, as the club's circular put it, to the 'terribly urgent struggle for World Peace & a better social & economic order & against fascism.' Texts were selected monthly by a small group with a strong communist presence and discussed in the local groups that formed, semi-spontaneously, to debate the issues, which were further explored in the Club's own publication, Left News. Most often cited were John Strachey's sequence of publications, from *The Coming Struggle for Power* onwards and popularisations of Marxist theory (Emile Burns, Herman Levy). Famously, George Orwell's *Road to Wigan Pier* was issued, with a carping preface by Gollancz himself, but, notoriously, his *Homage to Catalonia* was not.(Laity 2001).

And then there was Literature. Michael Roberts (himself a former communist) produced *New Country* (1933), an anthology of new work by young poets and writers of fiction – among them Day Lewis, Auden, Isherwood, Edward Upward, Stephen Spender and Charles Madge. In his contribution, 'Letter to a young revolutionary', Day Lewis called for: 'An absolute belief in revolution as the way to, and the form of, new life. This faith may come as an instantaneous flash; or a harvest, or a coral reef. But whether it grow quickly or slowly, it must come. You must have a conversion.' And he adds, 'you might as well know that a few of

Figure 12 **Soviet architecture.** The Zuev Workers' Club in Moscow, a much admired example of Soviet Constructivist architecture, was designed by Ilya Golosov and finished in 1928. (Photo: Wikipedia Commons Licence)

us poets, in our capacity of receiving stations, do detect the vibrations of new life in Communism.' Charles Madge in his Letter to the Intelligentsia, was brisker:

'Lenin, would you were living at this hour:
England has need of you, of the cold voice
That spoke beyond Time's passions, that expelled
All the half treasons of the mind in doubt.' (Roberts 1933: 232)

THE CRACKS IN THE PICTURE

But there were grounds for doubt, some of them good ones.
As early as 1933, there was the trial of British engineers from Metro-Vickers, charged with sabotage and convicted on flimsy evidence. Stalin's suppression of the Kulaks and the mass starvation that followed was known at the time, if dismissed as hostile propaganda.

Then from 1936 the more celebrated trials, in Moscow, of the Old Bolsheviks – and their confessions in court became increasingly hard for many independent observers to credit (though some did). The purges and consignment of dissenters to the gulag, where among millions of others Prince-Comrade Mirsky and other former comrades well known to the CPGB perished, must surely have created doubt among Party members, even while they dismissed the information as right-wing propaganda. However, Willie Thompson reports in his history of the Party, *The Good Old Cause*, that

'Conversations and discussions that I have had with people who were at the time mostly grass roots members, but occasionally in responsible positions result in a nearly universal claim that the trials evoked in their thinking very little doubt or apprehension and that they accepted the then official version unquestioningly because they were not very concerned about the issue. I have every confidence that these respondents were truthfully reporting what they

thought they remembered, but I am equally certain that their recollections of relative unawareness were playing them false and that a form of collective amnesia was at work.' (Thompson 1992: 62)

There is supporting testimony from Ralph Russell:

'To us in the Cambridge branch, imbued with so strong a sense of positive purpose in what we were doing, although the trials were disturbing there seemed to be no reason to doubt that the accused were guilty.' (2001:147)

All in all, this can be seen as a textbook example of the application of the doctrine of 'democratic centralism' in the management of the Party's affairs, by which a decision once reached by the legitimate central authority becomes an instruction to implement without further discussion or question.

And the same attitudes and behaviour were reflected in the increasingly virulent assault on 'Trotskyism' and its alleged manifestations – in Britain the ILP, in Spain the POUM (Partido Obrero de Unificación Marxista) – which the CPGB as a loyal member of the Comintern were under instructions to pursue.

And even after Munich (1938), the CPGB was still equivocating about rearmament, opposing conscription and less than clear about what the Party's position should be if war did break out. Would it be an imperialist war waged by a British government unworthy of support, or did the Party's often proclaimed duty to fight fascism take precedence, as Harry Pollitt would initially suggest?

Figure 13 **Mass Observation.** This report summarises some of Mass Observation's work before the Second World War, including reports from their 'observers' and their Worktown project in the North of England. (Photo: the authors)

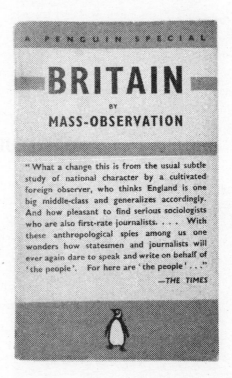

Figure 14   Left Book Club leaflet. (Photo: the authors)

IF

this little book has interested you

why not

JOIN THE LEFT BOOK CLUB?

Members of this Club (there are more than 50,000 of them) receive, at a price that is a mere fraction of that paid by the ordinary public, books of vital importance to you — for instance, the much bigger book *The Theory and Practice of Socialism* by John Strachey, the author of what you have just read : or that wonderful adventure book that explains what is going on in China, *Red Star Over China* : or a splendid complete new *History of England*, written from an up-to-date point of view.

Write for full particulars to

VICTOR GOLLANCZ, LIMITED

14 Henrietta Street, Covent Garden, London, W.C.2

Figure 15 **Left Book Club books.** This sample of Left Book Club publications shows the wide range of issues addressed in this successful left-wing propaganda exercise. (Photo – the authors)

Figure 16 **New Country.** This influential collection included both prose and poetry by many of the prominent writers associated with the left in the thirties. (Photo: author)

The Nazi-Soviet pact settled that question. The change of line laid down from Moscow – that the war was indeed imperialist and to be resisted – initially confused the Party and divided the small group whose experiences I have been following. But once the Central Committee of the CPGB had obediently swung behind the Comintern decision, many of them – though not all – also accepted it, obedient to the principle of democratic centralism.[6]

However, I don't propose to follow them after 1939. Most were swept up in the war and were then able after 1941 to relax into unconditional support for the USSR as Britain's now much-prized 'Soviet ally'.

IN SUMMARY

At one extreme the CPGB was a 'bed and breakfast' Party – membership was brief and engagement with Party activities a gesture not sustained, although the consequences in later life could be serious.

Some recruits found the level of commitment required was too great. Others encountered disapproval in their professional milieu and ceased to be active. Personal circumstances changed and the primary loyalty to the Party couldn't be sustained. But others remained Party members, if in some cases inactive ones, up to the demise of the CPGB in 1991.

Returning to the questions I asked at the beginning, the personal histories I've drawn upon don't suggest that this small group stood

6 Many members found this change easy enough to accept, though at least one of our group, Jack Gaster, didn't. Eric Hobsbawm comments that in accordance with precedents in communist parties outside power 'the leadership had to go through the process of repeating its case for the official line until there was no room for doubt about what we were expected to vote for (the technical term for this process was "patiently explaining"). After the vote, "democratic centralism" required that argument should give way to unanimous action' (Hobsbawm 2002: 135). Nevertheless, he believes that there was 'something heroic' in the way that the CPGB fell into line on receiving the Comintern's instructions.

out from their contemporaries in any very significant way – not in their characters, their relations with their families or their material circumstances or class situations. They shared many of the concerns and preoccupations of those politically aware young people at this period who wanted to do something about the problems their generation faced.

Rather, their decision to take the step of joining the CPGB, which distinguished them from the rest of their age group, was often driven by circumstance – the educational institutions they attended, their teachers, their fellow pupils; or experiencing fascism at first hand – in Nazi Germany, Austria and later Spain. And then there were individual encounters – personal friendships, meetings with plausible recruiters and sometimes sexual relationships.

To those who took this step it often seemed a natural thing to do: the reasoning appeared quite straightforward. As a member of the MI5 staff whose task was to explain after the war the prevalence of Party members in this age group commented in an internal minute:

'. . . the economic depression at home and the rise of fascism in Germany gave the communist movement a powerful attraction for many of the brighter undergraduates of the day.'(MI5 file (Meyer) 1951)

But there were, of course, also strong reasons for not taking that step and most of their contemporaries did not, though sometimes not without hesitation.

SOME LESSONS FROM EXPERIENCE

So what lessons can be drawn from the experiences of this perhaps not very typical group? And what judgments can be made about their decision to join the Party?

First, there's no doubt whatsoever that they cared about the issues of the day. This seems admirable; but there was always a danger of casting the net too wide. As Christopher Isherwood put it:

'I knew what I was supposed to feel, what it was fashionable for my generation to feel. We cared about everything: fascism in Germany and Italy, the seizure of Manchuria, Indian nationalism, then the Irish question, the Workers, the Negroes, the Jews. We had spread our feelings over the whole world; and I know that mine were spread very thin.' (1946: 105)

The great virtue, as far as the Party was concerned, of Spain as an issue was that it provided a unique focus for action – ranging from joining the International Brigade, nursing, through to fundraising for medical aid and refugee children and campaigning to change government policy on non-intervention. Spain became the 'good cause' of the decade and one on which communists could campaign – and recruit – without inhibition, alongside other progressives.

However, in joining the Party they relinquished at least some of their critical faculties. They had seen an image of the (radiant) future, whether literally, in the case of most of those who had travelled to the USSR, or at least in principle. The Party's political education classes, especially the study of Marxist-Leninist texts, set out an inevitable progression: the 'wave of the future'. Although the journey might present difficulties or raise awkward questions about the means that would have to be employed, the destination seemed not to be in doubt. Even though the precise form that a 'Soviet Britain' would assume remained less than clear.

This seems to be in part the reason why the events of the thirties that might have given pause for thought (the treason trials, the Gulag, the POUM episode and obsessional chasing of Trotskyists) did not have much impact on this group. Only the Nazi-Soviet pact in 1939 and the Party's embrace of 'revolutionary defeatism' gave some of them pause for thought.

But there was another side to this surrender to the authority of the Party and the democratic centralism of its decision taking, as in the change of line in 1939. There was also reassurance to be found in membership of a disciplined organisation and in the comradeship of Party members across class differences. As the CPGB liked to say, there was 'no rank and file in the Party', this meant equal share in the tasks and the rewards of participating in joint endeavours for common goals.

Comradeship transcended national boundaries and gave the British comrades ready access to local contacts and help when meeting fellow communists abroad; and impelled them in turn to make positive responses to the situation of foreign or overseas communists in Britain – whether exiles from Nazi Germany and Austria or from different parts of the British Empire.

As the anthem put it, the *Internationale* united the human race. The cultural mission of the British Party after the end of the 'class against class' period also produced some worthwhile outcomes. There was the response to Comintern insistence that national parties should rediscover what was useful in the radical past histories of their own countries. The various different cultural activities pushed forward by the Party – in art, architecture, theatre, cinema – were often vigorous and effective and not always crude agitprop. Festivals, pageants and other mass spectacles organised by Party members encouraged participation. Party literature, including the *Daily Worker*, became far more appealing both in presentation and content. (Bounds 2012)

Nevertheless, the achievements of the CPGB during the thirties, to which some middle-class recruits made significant contributions, must be seen as modest. The industrial wing of the Party, in which they were only marginally involved, made some progress but political gains, outside the Little Moscows of South Wales and Fife (and perhaps Hampstead?), were modest. The CPGB, far from being a mass Party, was at best, as Harry Pollitt liked to see it, the militant wing of the broader labour movement (which obstinately refused to accept it as such).

And, finally, there can and should be no doubt that the communism that this group adopted was based on an illusion. Not so much that the intellectual foundations on which it was built were unsound but that the structures that had been erected by Soviet communists upon them and imposed on the member parties of the Comintern were not liberating but confining. The young middle-class recruits of the 1930s cannot be blamed for not anticipating the dire consequences of Stalinism in the postwar world. But they can properly be reproached for not acknowledging what many of their contemporaries could see – that the seeds of totalitarianism were always present.

If that seems a negative note to end on, I would like to add that for me to encounter at first hand the idealism of this small group and their generation was in many respects a highly positive experience. If not the absolute brightest and best, they were somewhere close to it. It is difficult to avoid making some parallels with later generations of young idealists – the peace campaigners and the CND. And now we have groups of anti-capitalism protesters attempting to address another world economic crisis. But that's outside my brief and I'll leave it to others to pursue – should they wish to do so.

NOTE ON CASES AND SOURCES

For these lectures I have drawn on unpublished material about the experiences of a number of individuals mentioned in the text – Jack Gaster (papers in the Bishopsgate Institute) and his wife Maire Lynd (family papers), François Lafitte (papers in Birmingham University archive), Charles Madge (papers in University of Sussex archive) and Richard Clark and Mary McIntosh (family papers) – and an essay by their daughter Elizabeth Dolan about them, published below. James Klugmann is the subject of an essay (by Geoff Andrews) later in this collection. In addition, a number of individuals contributed material about their relatives at the final seminar, which are also included – Jane Bernal on her mother Margot Heinemann, Phil Cohen on his uncle Len Jones, Norma Cohen on her parents Eve and Eric and Hamish MacGibbon about his father James. I have had the benefit of helpful recollections by Jean McCrindle about her father Alex. The archivist of the Westminster School Archive, Elizabeth Wells, was particularly helpful, as were the staff of the People's History Museum, Manchester. I have also been able to draw upon the files of MI5 and the Metropolitan police held in the National Archive, among which several of my subjects and many other Party members of the period figured.

CHAPTER TWO: MIDDLE-CLASS RECRUITS TO COMMUNISM IN BRITAIN IN THE 1930s

KEVIN MORGAN

Attending the Fifth World Congress of the Communist International (or Comintern) in Moscow in 1924, delegates from Britain were asked to describe the work being carried out there among the middle classes. Their answer, literally in a word, was 'none.' Their Party – the Communist Party of Great Britain, or CPGB – was one of the Comintern's most solidly and unabashedly proletarian sections, and would remain so throughout the 1920s. It was also one of the smallest in proportion to the country's size and the very considerable resources which the Comintern devoted to it. Rooted in the old industrial Britain, in particular the declining staple industries, its high point of activity was the General Strike and miners' lockout of 1926. If students and ex-students played any part at all, it was generally as strike-breakers. Of the very few middle-class communists there were in Britain, most had been inherited from older political movements like guild socialism.

By the end of the 1930s the CPGB was a very different sort of animal. To begin with it was very much larger, and with nearly twenty thousand members by 1939 had experienced the first sustained membership growth of its history. What this also represented was the tapping into new sources of recruitment. The Party's fourteenth National Congress, held at Battersea in May 1937, was the most youthful in its seventy-one year history, with nearly half of the five hundred delegates aged under thirty. Well over half of them had been recruited since 1932, most of these in the three years since 1934. The CPGB retained a strong self-identity as a Party of the working class. Indeed, a veritable cult of the worker, particularly the sinewy, muscular male worker, can be found abundantly attested in the communist iconography of the time. At Battersea it was the older proletarian leaders who dominated the congress platform, and industrial employments alone are given specific consideration in the published congress report. The delegates themselves, however, present a rather different picture, for of those in paid employment nearly as many (152) worked in clerical and professional occupations as in industry (186) (CPGB 1937).

There were also thirteen students, as well as a now unquantifiable number of recent graduates to be found among the younger professional workers attending. Nevertheless, the idea of the middle class was not restricted in this period to the still extremely limited group that had had the opportunity of a university education. Even within this group, the communists of the day have been presented as a sort of gilded youth, not just 'the public-school undergraduate in revolt' but the better public schools at that (Harrison 1991; Wood 1959) .This is just one of the ways in which the experience of the 1930s has been oversimplified, if not actually misrepresented. Among the students, the public school component was giving way over the course of the decade to a grammar-school enrolment. Beyond this restricted environment, authors in or close to the Communist Party, like Alec Brown and Franz Klingender, reflected what for many contemporaries was an interest, preoccupation and even anxiety regarding what appeared to them to be a 'vast middle-class army, mainly of bureaucrats' caught between the 'far more numerous working class' and the 'steeply narrowing apex of the pyramid' represented by the bourgeoisie proper. (Brown 1936; Kligender 1935) This was also the 'sinking' middle class of Orwell's *Road to Wigan Pier*: 'The private schoolmaster, the half-starved freelance journalist, the jobless Cambridge graduate… the clerks, the civil servants, the commercial travellers …' (Orwell 1937). As Orwell famously put it, it was that class that had nothing to lose but its aitches.

The reason for this interest was the headlong expansion of the middle class to a size which communist leader Harry Pollitt estimated at some eleven million (CPGB 1938). The reason for their anxiety was that, as this class sank, or appeared to sink, it seemed to many the decisive social element in the rise of fascism, and the key to the wide political movement that had to be mobilised against it. This was the lesson, on the one hand, of the rise of Hitler, and, on the other, of the Popular Fronts that by the middle of the decade had been established in France and Spain. The issue could hardly have been starker, and the whole next phase of human history seemed to hinge on which way this class turned. The compulsion to take sides so characteristic of the 1930s is impossible to understand without a clear sense of how high the stakes seemed – and actually were. It is to this vaster middle class, and not just its social and cultural luminaries, that the new social complexion of communist parties must be traced, not just in Britain, but in France, Belgium, the USA and the other western democracies.

1930S RECRUITS – A NEW MIDDLE CLASS GENERATION

From these contrasting images of the 1920s and 1930s two simple observations follow. The first is that the middle-class communist in Britain was as much a generational as a social phenomenon, with a common generational identity that was above all bound up with anti-fascism and the war in Spain. It was the cold war rather than the war itself which brought it to a close, and the historian Edward Thompson observed that it was the early-to-mid 1940s that saw the greatest influx of intellectuals into Europe's communist parties (Thompson 1978). In the reflections of that other great historian to emerge from this milieu, Eric Hobsbawm, it is nevertheless impossible to miss the sense more specifically of a 1930s collective memory and sensibility. As Hobsbawm put it in defiance of all revisionist histories, Spain remained to him at the end of his life the only cause 'which, even in retrospect, appears as pure and compelling as it did in 1936' (Hobsbawm 2002).

Another 1930s recruit, Margot Kettle, produced a volume of interviews with contemporaries, *Recollections of a younger world*, which was to have come out on the fiftieth anniversary of the Spanish war. As yet it remains unpublished in the archives: like an album compiled for 'those born later', who, like the readers of Brecht's famous poem, might struggle to understand the harder choices that 'dark times' had required (Brecht 1979). As it happens, Brecht had also been writing in the years of the Spanish war, which synchronised so perfectly with Stalin's show trials. Thompson, on the other hand, joined the Party only in 1942, when communism had for the time being entered the political mainstream. The sense of a cause to be maintained in defiance of the odds had given way to a feeling of vindication and of the perspectives of social betterment now opening up for a post-war world. Already, Thompson and the wartime influx of communists may be regarded in some respects as the first of those generations 'born later' than the generation of the 1930s.

The other obvious point is that this was no single generational cohort and that the Party which these young people joined was one that was changing rapidly over time. Thompson's closest collaborator in later breaking with Stalinism, John Saville, was a Party recruit of 1934 vintage who referred to his as a generation quite distinct from Thompson's and marked by 'Spain, anti-appeasement and the Hunger Marches' (Morgan 1993). In life-history interviews with former communists, this was the sort of distinction that came out again and again, as relatively small differences in the time of joining the Party could often make a big difference in the sort of Party one joined. The sudden convulsions of communist policy – the proverbial Party 'line' – have long since been a matter of notoriety; usually linked with developments in the USSR, they are epitomised by the CPGB's volte-face over the issue of the war at the time of the Nazi-Soviet Pact in 1939. But there was also a more incremental change in the sort of social environment which the middle-class recruit encountered on crossing the Party threshold.

THE POPULAR FRONT – A TURNING POINT?

Partly this was also a matter of the 'line': that of the Popular Front approach, inaugurated in 1934-5, included an orientation towards the radicalised middle class that the communists of 1924 would scarcely have thought conceivable. It was also simply a matter of numbers, as increasingly these middle-class recruits began to encounter within the Party a critical mass of the sorts of people among whom they already lived, worked or studied. This was a development that was largely unaffected by the superficial reversion to more traditional Leninist positions at the time of the Nazi-Soviet Pact. Just as that dialectician Friedrich Engels had noted how quantitative change had at some point to become one of quality, so in some milieux, whether geographical or social, it was the middle-class character of British communism that some now began to remark upon. When Pollitt sought election for a South Wales mining constituency, it was on 'Posh Cars' and Oxford accents that his Labour opponents now turned their scorn. 'How these 'bright young things' enjoy the incursions amongst the workers, and what a 'thrill' to work for a Communist!' jeered a Labour election broadsheet. 'The paters probably regard it as a delightful way for the young dogs to expend their surplus energy.'

It was certainly very different from the forbidding and sometimes aggressively proletarian organisation that just a few years earlier had been found almost anywhere but the universities. Even in the universities, there was a shift away from what was initially a somewhat forthright revolutionism with distinctive mannerisms of language, dress and conduct. 'Far more "normal" young men were coming towards Communism', it was reported with obvious satisfaction, not in revolt against 'social convention or cultural emptiness', and still less, as Philip Toynbee put it, to avoid changing their shirts with greater regularity (Sloan 1938). Communists were not only urged to excel according to conventional criteria of the good student. In cases like that of Margot Kettle, they were literally indistinguishable as communists as a function of their assumption of a broader representative role – such as Kettle exercised as secretary of the National Union of Students (NUS). There was certainly no question, as in the case of Kettle's first husband Gabriel Carritt, of dropping one's given name for the proletarian 'Bill'. or seeking to flatten one's diphthongs as a way of dissimulating one's Pater – who in this instance was an Oxford philosophy don. 'I used to want to be working class', Carritt recalled a half-century later. 'I couldn't bear the fact that anybody should know what my background was.' Distinctions of cohort were no doubt particularly marked in the case of student communist parties whose membership was comprehensively renewed over the three-year undergraduate cycle. Even disregarding the war years, the 1930s recruits are perhaps best thought of as a series of overlapping cohorts with certain key defining experiences, of which the most indelible was usually Spain.

THE USSR: AN IDEAL SOCIETY?

Of course, there was also Russia. For those already making their way into the Party by the late 1920s, the key push factor was initially the Great Depression, compounded by the memory and the further

threat of war. Symptomatically, in Cambridge the watershed year of
1933-4 was marked on the one hand by the arrival of a contingent
of northern hunger marchers, and on the other by the organisation
by the communists of an anti-war exhibition that achieved a wide
publicity. But it was not just the hunger marches, nor yet the anti-
appeasement that combined so perplexingly with anti-war, but the
five-year plans and their assiduous promotion in the west that still at
this stage played a crucial role in the making of potential communists.
Through novels, films and the carefully contrived verisimilitude of
the camera lens, the USSR's achievement of well-being and social
optimism through modernity was taken as a literal representation of
reality, like a counterfoil to the documentary genres of a crisis-ridden
capitalism. 'Dovzhenko is a great director, but he couldn't make peasants
act that ecstasy', wrote the future poet laureate Cecil Day Lewis. He
was referring to the concluding scenes of Dovzhenko's beguiling but
utterly fantastical paean to collectivisation: Earth. 'I think that film
might work conversions, and … a few of us as poets, in our capacity of
receiving stations, do detect the vibrations of new life in Communism.'
(Roberts 1933) For a few years, not only poets but also scientists,
educationalists, welfare reformers and planners were among the many
whose antennae responded to the signals emitting from Moscow. The
workers' delegations of the 1920s did not cease; but through agencies
like Intourist and the Society of Cultural Relations, both individuals
and parties drawn from the middle classes sailed forth in increasing
numbers to witness the marvels of socialist construction at first hand.

There was more to this than just another way of idealising workers,
or Dovzhenko's peasants. For the offspring of a class apparently sunk
or sinking, what communist society also seemed to offer was the
opportunity to employ one's skills and talents for some meaningful
social purpose uncontaminated by tawdry commercial imperatives. It
was in this period that the veteran Fabian socialists Sidney and Beatrice

Webb emerged as among the most passionate devotees of what they saw as a new civilisation. Although their own formative experiences dated back some half a century, in Beatrice's incomparable diaries one finds recorded the visits paid the Webbs by this latest generation of socialists in whom they also vested their hopes for the future. 'All the clever younger men are going communist,' she recorded Harold Laski telling them in June 1933, and the following year described the visit of the physicist Patrick Blackett, who was later to have so important an influence on the 'white heat' of Harold Wilson's scientific revolution. Already in his thirties, Blackett described to the Webbs how all the younger scientists were now looking to the USSR as exemplar:

'The outlook for science in the European countries is not promising and latterly even the financial resources in the USA have dried up ... One of the first stages in [the] fight will be the suppression of free speech and free thought in capitalist countries and the growth of freedom and expression in the USSR – especially in respect to scientific questions. One of the main attractions of the USSR to scientific workers, is the greater respect paid them under Soviet Communism than under capitalism. In Great Britain the scientist has a bare living not comparable to that of the lawyer, the tradesman, the business manager. In the USSR he is relatively well paid. Moreover the Soviet scientist has unlimited equipment and a very generous allotment of assistants. Moreover adventuring and initiative are encouraged.'[7]

That Stalinism's allure might have lain in the promise of unfettered speech and thought must now seem difficult to credit. That capitalism seemed inimical to such values is not so extraordinary: not, at least, in view of the catastrophe which in Germany had just befallen what Roy Pascal, one of the earliest of the Cambridge communists, called 'the freest and most radical culture in the whole of the capitalist world'

---

7 The full version of the diaries is now fully accessible on-line via the website of the British Library of Political and Economic Science. The passages quoted date from 18 June 1933 and 26 July 1934.

(Pascal 1934). If capitalism teetered on the brink, fascism was what followed if it toppled. From Hitler's installation in power in 1933, it was the negative of the Nazi regime even more than the positive of Soviet communism that provided the sense of urgency and moral imperative that drew young people into active political engagements. It is from this period, and not just the war years, that the political ferment can be traced that was to culminate in Labour's political breakthrough in the 1945 general election.

ALTERNATIVES TO THE CPGB

It was not however only expressed through the Communist Party. Blackett, though he struck Beatrice as 'fanatically' pro-Soviet, was never to join. Day Lewis did, but only some years after first announcing his fascination with communism in verse. The impulses that led towards communism were felt in every European country in which they were allowed expression. Britain, however, had one of the smaller as well as more proletarian communist parties, and at the same time a broader labour movement culture that was remarkably accommodating of leftist and pro-Soviet views. There were therefore other channels through which positions not dissimilar to the communists' could be adopted, including established political formations as well as cultural and professional networks. Though it disaffiliated from the Labour Party in 1932, the Independent Labour Party (ILP) was still a force in the early 1930s. The Socialist League, representing those who wished to remain within the Labour Party, was vigorous in promulgating left-wing views, while the active and militant Labour League of Youth (LLY) was to test the limits of the Labour Party's disciplines almost to breaking point. Even among the Fabians, the Webbs' intoxication with Stalin was matched by their fellow veteran Bernard Shaw, whose writings were as influential on this younger generation as those of any author, not excluding Marx or Lenin.

In respect of these different left groupings, the story of the 1930s is that of the Communist Party's progressive advancement at the expense of its main competitors. Specifically in respect of its middle-class recruits, the transition to the Popular Front was a precondition for such a development. In previous years the skills and assets of its middle-class adherents had been undervalued if not a positive cause for suspicion. Further securing the Party against traditional forms of social advantage, Moscow's International Lenin School (ILS) turned out a steady supply of working-class activists whose induction into Leninist codes and disciplines gave them a prior claim to leadership roles and oversight.

RECRUITMENT IN THE UNIVERSITIES

Already by the early 1930s, the first communist groups in the universities had begun to appear. By April 1933, the Party's student secretariat reported 155 members, a more than doubling in the previous six months, with a focus on work in the university itself except in Oxford and Cambridge. A key figure in this period was the Cambridge economist Maurice Dobb, a Party member since 1922, who believed the opportunity existed for some wider association of Marxist intellectuals. Nevertheless, the attempt to set up an intellectual quarterly was for the time being thwarted, and in the Party press Dobb's own books were alternately patronised and savaged by ILS alumni. In the words of R. Palme Dutt, the CPGB's guardian of Bolshevik orthodoxy, there was no special sphere of work for the 'bourgeois intellectual strata,' and that remained true of the middle class more generally. Except in moments of 'necessary self-criticism'. as Dutt put it in 1932, the intellectual was to 'forget that he is an intellectual … and remember only that he is a Communist'. Formally speaking, the adoption of a broader Popular Front approach is usually dated from the Comintern's Seventh World Congress in the summer of 1935. Historian Steve Parsons has suggested that a feedback meeting on 'Professional workers and the World Congress' was the first such meeting of middle-class workers to be officially promoted by the CPGB. In practice, the new approach can nevertheless be seen emerging already with the first mobilisations around fascism and the Reichstag fire trial in the latter months of 1933. As the political catalyst of anti-fascism coincided with a more accommodating conception of the role of Party members, there was an upsurge of membership in the universities and a period of continuous expansion among the wider middle class.

SMALL NUMBERS – WIDER INFLUENCE

Three features of the Popular Front were crucial to the new phenomenon of middle-class communism. One was the emphasis on all Party members, whatever their occupation and background, working through broader movements where they lived and worked in order to maximise the CPGB's influence and campaigning impact. Already there were several of the so-called front organisations; the Labour Party, in proscribing them, referred to them as the communists' 'solar system'. Over the course of the 1930s there nevertheless emerged a plethora of publications, campaigns and institutions, many of them directly addressed to what was now allowed to be the 'special sphere' of work among professional or cultural workers. By 1938, not only had a *Modern Quarterly* appeared, more or less as Dobb had envisaged it. There were also Marx House, Unity Theatre, the Artists' International Association and numerous bodies concerned with international issues and the threats of fascism and war.

Above all, from 1936 there was the hugely successful Left Book Club (LBC), with a membership some three times that of the CPGB itself. It was not until after the war that the Party established a National Cultural Committee with oversight of a network of professional groups and activities of the Party itself. Already in the LBC, there were nevertheless poets, artists, doctors, scientists and similar groups that prefigured these later developments. Even in the universities, where communists were for some years the numerically predominant element among politically active students, they tended to work through broader-based bodies like the University Labour Federation (ULF) – which to all intents and purposes they controlled. Nor should one overlook how the CPGB's strong trade union orientation encouraged an active engagement with white-collar and professional unions, in many of which communists went on to play a formative or leading role. This, for example, was notably true of unions of clerks, teachers, scientific workers, building technicians and civil servants.

Also characteristic of the Popular Front period was the public recognition that was now extended to communism's middle-class standard bearers, as a sort of exemplification of the communists' claim to occupy a leading role in the defence of culture against barbarism. This new-found prominence is strikingly evident in the case of the Spanish civil war. The great majority of the two thousand or so Britons who fought in Spain were from working-class backgrounds, and often they were collectively represented as such. Nevertheless, in the individual memorialisation of those who died there, a disproportionate focus fell on those of the middle class. This was true, for example, of the three notable memorial volumes produced during the period of the war itself, and dedicated to the relative Party veteran, Ralph Fox, and two much younger figures, David Haden Guest and John Cornford.

Cornford is perhaps the best known of these. His poems have been widely anthologised, and having died at the age of twenty-one, still very much the student communist leader, he was at once a hero, martyr and role model for the student communists of the time. In some ways it is Fox's case that is nevertheless more revealing. Like Dobb, Fox had already joined the CPGB in the early 1920s. Educated at Oxford and the Sorbonne, he was the author of several novels and biographies and might have expected recognition as one of Britain's most gifted left-wing writers. Nevertheless, it was only in the last phase of his life that his talents began to be regarded as a positive asset to be exploited, and in his unstinting commitment to the Party Fox had for many years been confined to essentially second-level tasks. Only on his death, at Cordova in January 1937, was he finally installed as a sort of symbol of 'the alliance between mental and manual worker' in defence of culture (Lehmann et al 1937).

The very titles of the Spanish memorial volumes – *A Writer in Arms, A Scientist Fights for Freedom* – suggest a validation and celebration of the values represented by such figures. By contrast, the diminution of Comintern subsidies over the decade may at first seem to have a somewhat tangential connection to these middle-class recruits. Even so, it was the substantial support received in both cash and kind from Moscow that, since the origins of the CPGB, had provided the material basis for its robustly proletarian ethos and helped keep the likes of Fox in their place. In a period of continuous mass unemployment in the older industrial areas from which the Party had mainly recruited, working-class activists whom victimisation and blacklisting had often excluded from conventional employments were thus enabled to take on political responsibilities from which they would otherwise have been excluded by their material circumstances. As these subventions were scaled down during the 1930s, there consequently followed a reversion to the more familiar conventions of British politics by which time and social capital were contributed by those who had the opportunity to do so. In a sense, the Spanish memorial volumes were a symptom of that; it was 'family circumstances', Pollitt wrote in one of them, that prevented the greater number of working-class volunteers being commemorated in the same way.(Haden Guest 1939) .The effectiveness of popular-front communism nevertheless owed a good deal to the young and passionately committed middle-class recruits who provided the ill-paid or voluntary workers on which so many of the period's campaigns depended.

In social terms, the parallel was sometimes noted with an older Fabian socialist tradition that by this time was half a century old. The Fabians too had always been low on numbers, but made up for it through the willingness to take on wider responsibilities which was so central to their strategy of permeation. Epitomising the continuities between the two traditions was the Fabian Research Department, now the Labour Research Department (LRD), which the Webbs had launched two decades earlier and which under communist direction provided the same unsung activities of servicing the labour movement through information and technical support. Prominent LRD workers and volunteers included Margot Heinemann, to whom Cornford in Spain had inscribed one of the century's most beautiful love poems, and Noreen Branson, who sixty years later was still working for the department in an entirely voluntary capacity. Roger Simon was another long-time voluntary worker, whose father Ernest Simon had been a keen supporter of the Webbs financially and supported the LRD in its Fabian inception. Brought up in an 'atmosphere of public service,' both Roger and his brother Brian, the well-known educationalist, transmuted this into a commitment to communism which in both their cases lasted a lifetime.

Historians have often located the Popular Front within a longer progressive tradition, and communism may to this extent be regarded as one of the characteristic vehicles of these commitments for those politicised in the 1930s. At the same time, in the temporary confluence of these traditions and those deriving from the Russian revolution there were also obvious differences. What to many was part of the compelling attraction of communism in a decade of crisis was what also came to seem jejune or even sinister as the crisis passed. For every communist who, like the stalwarts at the LRD, stayed the course, there was another who found some other outlet for the ideals they had believed it embodied, and a third who came to regard it as the proverbial 'god that failed'[8].

Of the distinctive features of the phenomenon, the two that most caused embarrassment or controversy were a penchant for conspiratorialism and the association with an international movement that was centred in Moscow. Fabian socialists, to reflect for a moment on the conspiratorial aspect, had not usually declined to identify themselves as such. Nor were they accountable for their activities to any Party apparatus, let alone one functioning according to the precepts of democratic centralism. It is also easy to overstate the degree of oversight which the Communist Party itself exercised. Though the Comintern had built up a formidable machinery of control and communications, it was badly hit by Stalin's terror. In Britain, the Party organisation did not keep pace with the influx of new members. Forms of association were often surprisingly informal; control in these cases was achieved through self-discipline, and co-ordination as much as anything by the

---

8 The title of a collection of personal testimonies of disillusionment edited by the Labour MP Richard Crossman and published in 1949.

continuous updating in the communists' changing world-view that the *Daily Worker* had since 1930 provided.

Nevertheless, one of the features of the period was a widespread acceptance of the practice of a form of undercover membership. Anti-commnunism was a real force in society, and for some middle-class members, career or employment interests enjoined discretion. In due course a 'commercial branch' was set up of Jewish Party members with business interests, whose identity was known only to King Street. In a period in which the Labour Party sought to stifle common action with communists, others were primarily concerned to avoid political proscriptions. In many cases – the sort who tried to sell you the *Daily Worker* – political preferences were an open secret. Others, however, functioned in the more decidedly conspiratorial way which they described as that of the mole. When in 1939, Gabriel Carritt stood as a Westminster by-election candidate supported by Sir Richard Acland and the local Labour and Liberal parties, neither he, they nor the voters knew that 'independent progressive' actually meant a communist. [9]

In respect of movements of which communists were the instigators or principal animators, which in this period included quite a few local trade union organisations and Labour parties, it is difficult to think of this simply as infiltration. Nevertheless, for the younger recruit in particular, this entrustment with a code of secrecy served to reinforce and even glamorise the sense of admission to a great fraternity. On some broad platforms of the youth and student movement, every major grouping – the LLY, ULF, British Youth Peace Assembly – might be represented by a communist. Margot Kettle had already worked for the League of Nations Union before moving onto the NUS. 'We didn't feel we were cheating', she insisted long afterwards. 'We just thought

---

9 The election was in the Westminster Abbey division and Carritt obtained nearly a third of the vote.

it would make it easier for people to appreciate what we were trying to do if they didn't get this hang-up about communism.' For many, and probably most, this was a specifically 1930s experience, exposed with dramatic effect (but no real sense of surprise) when some hundreds of these figures announced their ostensible conversion to the Communist Party in the period of the Nazi-Soviet pact. For those like Kettle who did not do so, even in the more benign political environment of the latter war years, the designation crypto-communist was aptly coined.

INTERNATIONALISM: SOLIDARITY AND SPYING

The sense of belonging to an international movement was another distinguishing feature and one of communism's most basic attractions. Often it is discussed as if this only meant the USSR. According again to Hobsbawm, it is true that those who committed to communism in the early 1930s may still be regarded as the tail-end of a founding generation for whom Russia and the October Revolution were the central point of reference (Hobsbawm 2002). Though loyalty to an idealised USSR persisted, increasingly it was not only located within a wider set of international commitments but also overshadowed by them. 'I was waking up in the morning thinking in Spanish', recalled the pianist James Gibb, and Spain in particular was for a period a primary focus of left-wing hopes and forebodings. Few then could have conceived of the sheer scale and human cost of Stalin's terror. Nevertheless, even its public face of leader worship and show trials was hardly the material one needed in campaigning for the 'defence of culture.' The open door to western well-wishers was in any case now barely ajar, and the unnegotiable commitment to the USSR now receded somewhat from its earlier predominance in communist propaganda.

For a small number, conspiratorialism and pro-Sovietism came together in the spying activities which have provided what is probably the most widely circulated image of the middle-class communists of the 1930s. In respecting the intention not to get drawn into this debate, certain reflections are nevertheless germane to the broader themes of the seminar. One is that these widely-publicised cases, not infrequently identified on an evidential basis that would not pass muster in any other field of history, are anything but typical and can hardly represent the wider experience of the 1930s. On the other hand, there was little in the culture of the Communist Party that would have inclined one to the disapproval or repudiation of such activities, except inasmuch as they rebounded on the Party itself. As Hobsbawm (2002) once more put it, lines of loyalty 'ran not between but across countries', and this was indeed a basic principle of socialist internationalism. George Barnard, later a prominent statistician, recalled his disgust at learning that Guy Burgess had reverted to type in taking his place among the conservative echelons of the British establishment. When afterwards Burgess was exposed as a spy, Barnard felt that he owed him an apology. More generally, there is no real evidence of any communist feeling of revulsion or disillusionment on learning of the Burgess and Maclean case. What did produce revulsion for some thousands, among whom the middle-class recruits of the 1930s were especially prominent, was the acknowledgement by Khrushchev that the regime they were spying for was a monstrous tyranny.

Politically, joining the Communist Party was often a life-changing moment, and manifestly so for those who never broke with the Party. Socially, the picture is not nearly so clear-cut. Class divisions in the 1930s ran deep in Britain: one need only think of the old Etonian Orwell wandering around Wigan, or the anthropologist Tom Harrisson who returned from the 'savage civilisation' he found in Borneo to mass-observe another one, only somewhat less exotic, in Bolton. There is no doubt that part of the Communist Party's attraction was as a social environment in which these distinctions appeared to be surmounted. For some, escaping from the world of 'mate' or 'sir' was symbolised by the universal appelation 'comrade'. Advised by R. Palme Dutt, the critic Alick West was one of a sizeable group of middle-class communists who took the positive decision to move to a more proletarian district. Another of the period's recruits described it as 'get[ting] out of one class skin and into another.'

That was in 1942, when the shaking up of settled arrangements through diverse forms of war service certainly did bring about a broadening of horizons, one that was by no means confined to communists but which did nevertheless play its part in the trebling of the Party's membership in this period. In the absence of such external pressures, the Popular Front emphasis on activity within one's own work or social environment did nevertheless lead to the establishment of distinctly middle-class networks within the CPGB. In the post-war period, this was formalised in the work of the Party's professional groups, like the very successful teachers' group. Even in the 1930s, one of the most revealing ways of approaching this is to look at where communists found their marriage partners. There were certainly examples of what, in class terms, might be regarded as 'marrying out'. Primarily these were middle-class women, typically teachers, who married the male industrial workers, some of them now Party functionaries, who bore the masculinist kudos of the worker so central to the Party's identity. Even so, communists did by and large find their partners among the same social groups as if they had not been communists, and it is especially unusual to find examples of a partnership between a professional man and working-class woman. For the oral historian of a later period, on visiting the homes of these 1930s recruits it was also abundantly clear that the movement into less middle-class residential environments had, for the most part, been a temporary phenomenon.

It is in any case misleading to associate communism, even middle-class communism, with a form of downward mobility. On the contrary, what is striking in so many communist life-histories is how the experience of Party membership is described less in terms of self-denial in a greater cause than of what the Webbs would have called the 'expansion of personality'. Sociologists seeking to explain working-class militancy have often employed the notion of blocked mobility; that is, they describe how the entrapment of gifted and highly motivated individuals within alienating or restrictive work situations can have a politically radicalising effect, as these energies find an outlet in some other form of activity. It would obviously be absurd to extend these notions to a figure like Roger Simon, declining to take his seat in the House of Lords and prioritising his commitments to the LRD. On the other hand, if we think again of that larger middle class, eleven million strong, it reminds us of a world of white-collar employments which in many cases provided only a deadening sense of hierarchical, exploitative and often socially useless or pernicious work. Women in particular might be restricted in terms of both work and educational opportunities, sometimes in comparison with their own siblings.

Retrospective testimonies provide abundant confirmation of how important this experience could be. For the middle-class communists of the 1930s there were to be many potential disillusionments, from the Nazi-Soviet Pact, through the revelations of 1956, to the crushing of the Prague Spring, which stifled any last hope of a reform communism. It is not surprising that so many accounts of former communists express not only disillusionment but also real bitterness regarding Stalinism and sometimes the Communist Party itself. But what is also striking is how very much rarer it is that the experience of Party membership itself is described in negative terms. Thompson (1979) referred to it as the 'complex and contradictory' character of the communist movement, with its inherent tension between a rigid organisation and political orthodoxy and the 'innumerable voluntary initiatives' that were often of a profoundly democratic character. It is precisely this complex and contradictory character that makes the phenomenon so difficult to sum up in a short paper.

NOTE

This is a slightly expanded version of my talk at Gresham College. Readers interested in a fuller discussion of these themes are referred to my *Communists in British Society 1920-1991* (with Gidon Cohen and Andrew Flinn, 2007) and 'Socialists and mobility in twentieth-century Britain: images and experiences in the life-histories of British communists', *Social History*, vol. 36, no. 2 (2011). *Socialist History* no. 24 (2002) was a special issue on *'Interesting times'* including an interview with Eric Hobsbawm and reminiscences of Cambridge communists of the 1930s and early 1940s. It can be obtained through the Socialist History Society website.

CHAPTER THREE: JAMES KLUGMANN

GEOFF ANDREWS

'For my mother's generation,' the late Raphael Samuel has written, 'communism, though not intended as such, was a way of being English, a bridge by which the children of the ghetto entered the national culture. It was also, in some sense, a break, from hereditary upbringing, as my mother put it, 'to emancipate ourselves from the narrowness of a religious environment' (Samuel 2006). James Klugmann was of the same generation as Minna Nirenstein, Raphael Samuel's mother, and his own route to communism during the late 1920s and early 1930s while at school and university also involved breaking from family and religious pressures in the search for principles to live by. Joining the Communist Party, moreover, for him and others of his generation, was akin to belonging to a new family – as well as, in a different way, a new religion – and throughout his subsequent life and career was subject to the constraints, conflicts of loyalties and divisions characteristic of familial relations.

EARLY INFLUENCES: FAMILY AND SCHOOL

However Klugmann was not a 'child of the ghetto'. His father, Samuel, who had become a naturalised British subject in 1894 after arriving in this country as a young man from Germany, worked as a rope and twine merchant with an office in the City, while his mother, Anna Browne Rosenheim, was from a wealthy family of tea and wine merchants, who were already established in the middle class Belsize Park area of North London where he grew up. In fact, Klugmann had a seemingly impeccable Jewish bourgeois background. His parents both belonged to one of the more open-minded synagogues and his father, anxious to be accepted by the prosperous business community, was keen that his children received the sort of liberal education that might enable their entry into a comfortable middle class world. Unknowingly, his father's liberal aspirations opened up a quite different prospect for his two children: Karoline 'Kitty' Klugmann and her younger brother Norman, as he was still known in his early years; one which would bring family tensions and divisions that would never be fully resolved. His Jewish identity, moreover, became increasingly subsumed as his political identity as a communist took shape.

His elder sister Kitty was the first to benefit from Mr Klugmann's liberalism, as one of the first pupils at the re-launched Kingsley School, conveniently situated at 46 Belsize Park at the top of the Klugmann's large Lancaster Road house. Four years older than her brother, Kitty was to become a leading influence on his political development, as well as helping to initiate him into the wider world of the Party at Cambridge. Later, she and her husband, the communist philosopher Maurice Cornforth, would set up house together with her brother. Like many communist women, Kitty's own intellectual contribution has received little attention from historians and though her later endeavours as a Party worker have been acknowledged, her intellectual contribution has gone unrecognised; she is normally regarded as sister and wife of two prominent communist intellectuals.

Kingsley School's founding statement in 1890 declared that it was 'For the Daughters of Gentlemen and Doctors.' This would have appealed to the Klugmanns, but on reopening in 1915 it had the new leadership of philosopher Susan Stebbing (who would later become the first woman British professor of philosophy), along with her sister and two friends. Kitty joined the school the following year and she thrived in the new atmosphere; its horizons extended well beyond those of her kindergarten, and it was an exciting if uncertain time to be at the school in the midst of the First World War and with growing demands for women's suffrage. Smaller and without the prestige of nearby South Hampstead School for Girls, it nevertheless had high principles and a strong sense of community, with a third of its pupils from Jewish backgrounds. Through Stebbing and her fellow teachers, Kitty was introduced to many new ideas and interests. Stebbing herself taught 'Logic, Ethics, and Principles of Criticism'; in the words of one of Kitty's contemporaries, she 'taught you how to think, not what to think', and her determination that the girls should be encouraged to question orthodoxies was borne out through challenging the associations between pacifism and cowardice in the case of the conscientious objectors, considering seriously the arguments of the suffragettes and, towards the end of her time at the school, the rights of the strikers during the General Strike.

Kitty was also encouraged to think critically about the role of the British Empire by her young history teacher Kay Beauchamp. Beauchamp, already by then an active communist, would go on to be a leading campaigner against racism and imperialism and was a formative influence in Kitty's later decision at university to become a communist. Stebbing's influence remained pivotal however and under her influence Kitty won a scholarship to Girton College Cambridge to study moral sciences.

Kitty's last year at Kingsley School was her brother's last year at The Hall, a more established boys prep school, situated directly opposite Kingsley, where he had been since 1919. It was the year of the General Strike and the two would have had animated conversations about the implications of that event as they made their way to and from classes. Klugmann had excelled at The Hall, coming top in most subjects and earning the accolade from his headmaster that 'he is one of the cleverest boys we have ever had at The Hall.'[10]

He also thrived in the wider life of the school, editing, along with his cousin, Charles Rosenheim, the school magazine *The Upper Sixth Former*. It was here that he was able to develop his interest in current and world affairs, as well as gaining his first experience of editing, something that would occupy much of his later career as a communist intellectual. Extra-curricular school interests also included chess, and a penchant for political satire, and poetry; poignantly, one of his poems depicted the protagonists of the General Strike of 1926, a topic that would later form the basis of one of his history books.

The Hall School provided Klugmann with a comfortable, safe and perhaps secluded environment, close to home and family, with his influential sister and like-minded cousin in close proximity. His school success was nevertheless remarkable and should have raised his esteem and confidence ahead of his arrival at Gresham's School, Holt, in the autumn of 1926.

Gresham's had established itself as a liberal and progressive school, initially under the leadership of George Howson and, following his death in 1919, J.R.Eccles. Howson had transformed the status of the school and introduced the so-called 'honour' system which rejected corporal punishment in favour of placing trust in the pupils' honesty and loyalty to the school and their fellows. Eccles continued this tradition, by which time the school had caught the attention of many prominent liberal families, meaning that Klugmann's contemporaries included David Layton, son of Walter Layton, editor of *The Economist*, Roger and Brian Simon, sons of Ernest Simon, who as Baron Simon of Wythenshawe, was a notable liberal peer and reformer; Donald Maclean son of Sir Donald Maclean, Liberal Party politician and

---

10 Headmaster's Report, The Hall School, July 1926, p. 179

President of the Board of Education, and Peter and Bernard Floud, whose father was a British diplomat and senior civil servant. Eccles was delighted to have won the interest of such prominent parents with a strong commitment to the kind of civic ethics and public-spirited citizenship he shared and they were regularly invited to give talks and participate in the wider life of the school. Eccles selected the pupils of the most influential parents as members of his own house, Woodlands.

Despite his excellent academic record at The Hall, Klugmann found himself in Kenwynne House, one normally reserved for day boarders and the less academically gifted. His parents, their prosperous business interests and high aspirations for their children notwithstanding, could not compete with the public roles of some of the country's leading statesmen. Klugmann's two older cousins, Frank Norman and John Donald Klugmann, had been in Kenwynne, and this may be another reason why he started his Gresham's career there.

This must have increased his sense of isolation, however, as a young Jewish boy, hopeless at games and without the self-confidence of some of his more illustrious peers. He had little in common with his rugby-playing cousins, soon to embark on the career in the family business that he himself later rejected and, on his own admission, felt an 'oddity', an 'outsider', from the school. He continued to excel academically but he felt this only increased the perception of him as an oddball. In his early years at the school he lacked the speaking skills or the confidence to impose his ideas that would later come to define his role as a Party intellectual and talent-spotter. Indeed his own decision to call himself a communist was partly influenced by his isolation from the school and the rebellious feelings it generated.

'When I was at Gresham's, I felt so much out of things as the clever oddity who got most of the prizes, but not even the humblest office, that I cast around for a title to bestow on myself. I hit on an ingenious one in my last year, and I surmised at once that the authorities wouldn't like it. They certainly *didn't. For I called myself 'The Communist', advertising myself as the only specimen for miles around. I hadn't any clear idea, to begin with, what a good Communist really stood for; but having a very inquisitive mind, I soon remedied that. The books I read opened my eyes a little. Being also one of nature's rebels, I became a distant sympathiser.' (Boyle 1979)*

However, he found a kindred spirit and a mentor who would be his first significant influence beyond his family in Frank McEachran, the brilliant, eccentric French master. McEachran, then in his mid-twenties, though nominally teaching French, had an expansive range of interests which extended well beyond the curriculum and was wont to adopt unusual teaching methods, which often included getting students to recite 'spells'; extracts of poetry and prose. He would later leave Gresham's under a cloud and re-emerge at Shrewsbury School, where he spent the majority of his teaching career, and included several of the Private Eye generation among his pupils. He would be the model for 'Hector' in Alan Bennett's *The History Boys*. W.H. Auden had been at Gresham's and a pupil of McEachran immediately before Klugmann's arrival and he, like his tutor, found the honour system oppressive.

'It meant that the whole of our moral life was based on fear, or fear of the community, not to mention the temptation it offered to the natural informer, and fear is not a healthy basis. It makes one furtive and dishonest and unadventurous. The best reason I have for opposing Fascism is that at school I lived in a fascist state.' (Greene 1934)

The implicit requirement that pupils 'self-police' and report on their fellows inevitably gave rise to emotional torments and conflicts of loyalties, and this was a view largely shared by McEachran, and by Klugmann.

McEachran introduced James Klugmann to the world of history and philosophy, and nurtured his radicalism by imbibing him with a set of values to live by, including the importance of holding a 'worldview', or an 'outlook', to use one of Klugmann's own later favourite expressions. He instilled in him a love of history, and the belief that the values of European culture and civilisation, and notably the French Enlightenment, held the key to progress. It was through this route that Klugmann came to Marxism, and in his own teaching and writings, maintained that the revolution was in essence a continuation of those values – 'forward from liberalism' as he and his Cambridge communist comrades would argue.

At the beginning of the 1930s, as Europe entered its darkest hour, McEachran championed liberal humanism and his belief in the capacity of European culture to unify nations and peoples was optimistic, indeed utopian. Yet he went beyond defending the liberal tradition – then in crisis – and warned of the dangers of nationalism and romanticism which threatened to divide Europe.

This had significant influence on Klugmann and opposition to war became one of his early political actions, joining with Benjamin Britten, another of his contemporaries, who would be a lifelong pacifist[11] and a conscientious objector in World War II, David Layton, and others in refusing to join the Officer Training Corps. The recent memory of the First World War cast a shadow over Gresham's, which lost a hundred of its former pupils, and stimulated among the new generation an interest in peace and international affairs which resulted in its joining the League of Nations Union – the first British public school to do so.

These debates took on increased urgency in two other school forums – *The Grasshopper* magazine, set up by McEachran, and the school Debating Society. In the former, Klugmann contributed short stories on the modern condition of man. He was a regular participant in the Debating Society, with growing confidence in public speaking and the knowledge and intellect to defend his corner. Klugmann's contributions

---

11 Benjamin Britten's pacifism has been explored by Adam Roberts in his centenary essay, 'No jingo! Benjamin Britten and pacifism.' *Times Literary Supplement*, 22.11.2013

to debates included an attack on the distortion of European culture. 'Modern man,' he argued, 'had lost his sense of values and was treating soap and machinery as ends in themselves, instead of as means to a fuller and more satisfying experience.'[12]

It was in this context, and the increasingly intense political conversations in the library and in study bedrooms, that he formed close friendships and loyalties that would continue over long periods, in left wing student politics or, in the case of the Simon brothers, over a lifetime of Communist Party commitment. His closest friendship was with Donald Maclean, one that prospered in the vacations with visits to cinemas and bookshops and would continue at Cambridge. Klugmann's grasp of history and theory, together with his political acumen, would put him in the role of mentor to many of his student allies and Maclean was the first real example of this. The younger, more outspoken but volatile son of a liberal parliamentarian, had been drawn to Marxism but was uncertain of what its political ramifications might be. He looked to his older friend for political advice and support. It was a friendship – as I argue elsewhere[13] – which fostered loyalties and commitments that started at school, continued at Cambridge and ended in Moscow.

12   Debating Society minutes, 11 October 1930. All the debates were reported in detail in *The Gresham Magazine*, available from school archives.

13   My forthcoming biography of James Klugmann, *The Shadow Man: at the heart of the Cambridge spy circle.*, is to be published by I B Tauris in 2015

Klugmann, like Maclean, won a scholarship to Cambridge to study modern languages, at Trinity College and Trinity Hall respectively. Cambridge University, when he arrived in 1931, was far removed from radicalism of any sort, with its austere, conservative and hierarchical culture. Student politics, if anything, belonged to the right, with fresh recent memories of undergraduates driving buses and trams during the General Strike.

Klugmann knew all this from Kitty, who had been a brilliant philosophy (moral sciences) student and had recently returned from a year at Columbia University. She had also married Maurice Cornforth, a fellow philosophy student and pupil of Wittgenstein, who had helped establish the first organised communist student branch at Cambridge with his fellow philosopher and mathematician David Haden Guest, the previous spring. Prior to that the Communist Party at Cambridge relied on Maurice Dobb, the economics don, for putting forward the policy, and it did not take student politics seriously. It was an important, if modest, step in establishing a communist presence at the university and was helped by the Cornforths taking on the organisation of the town branch. The formation of the October Club at Oxford the following year and developments in other colleges increased the Party's presence among students.

Klugmann himself did not officially join the Party until 1933. This is surprising, given that he had committed time and energy to the cause during the previous two years. He had even hosted a major meeting of leading student communists and Party officials at his Hampstead home over Easter 1932, when his parents were away. That meeting was crucial in getting the National Student Bureau off the ground, and for the first time brought him to the attention of the Party leadership at King Street. It was not unusual for people to be active in and around the Communist Party without joining; much communist activity at this time continued to take place secretly with a conspiratorial air, and many were not open communists.

However, in Klugmann's case his reluctance to join the Party officially is partly explained by familial constraints. It is worth noting that despite being on the verge of the most radical period in student politics to date, his generation still deferred to parental authority on occasion. Like Maclean who, as the son of a leading Liberal Party parliamentarian, went through much angst in his own decision to finally join the Party after his father's death, Klugmann did not join while his father was alive. His and his sister's interest in communism had caused big rows with Samuel Klugmann, a solid Liberal Party supporter until the 1931 election when he voted Labour for the one and only time. ('It did him no good,' his son later remarked). His mother remained largely apolitical and never fully understood her children's politics.

He eventually joined shortly after his twenty-first birthday, as Hitler's rise to power intensified. The anti-fascist and anti-war activities galvanised the student left in Cambridge, much of which was organised by communists within the Cambridge University Socialist Society (CUSS), a broad umbrella organisation of the left, with communists exerting the leading influence. Immediately after joining, however, he was sent to the Rhondda Valley in South Wales to stay with unemployed miners during the Easter vacation of 1933. This had become the usual initiation for young middle-class communists like Klugmann; as for others, the visit was his first real experience of working-class life (the visits of Gresham's Sociological Society to witness the London poor paled in comparison). The trip had a profound effect on him and cemented the centrality of class in his political analysis, as well as preparing him for the arrival of the Hunger Marchers who would reach Cambridge the following year.

Back at Cambridge he joined David Haden Guest in the leadership of the student communists. Guest, who had been to Germany and experienced two weeks in jail after taking part in anti-fascist protests, was an energetic, single-minded campaigner, and he and the softly spoken Klugmann made an ideal organising partnership, spending long hours in student rooms patiently making the case that only communists had the answers to the ensuing economic and political crisis. Guest left Cambridge in the summer of that year and was later to die fighting in Spain.

The catalyst for the transformation of the Cambridge Left however was the arrival of John Cornford in October of that year. Cornford, the son of Cambridge academic parents, was a precocious student of history and poetry and an outspoken radical since his schooldays at Stowe. He had spent two terms at the London School of Economics, where he came under the influence of Frank Strauss Meyer, a wealthy American post-graduate student and founder of the October Club, who would be expelled by William Beveridge, the LSE's Director, for his political activities. Already active in a range of student groups (he was editor of *Student Vanguard*) and with early experience of addressing trade unionists behind him, Cornford was another energetic campaigner and organiser, and his close relationship with the older Klugmann was an ideal combination for the needs of the moment. Together, they built up the communist student presence through intense rounds of political meetings, with Cornford often at his best in the town activities and Klugmann impressing with his intellect, range and persuasive skills in small conversational gatherings in college rooms. Together, from their base at Trinity College (which was the core of the communist student organisation) they brought a serious strategy and commitment to communist activities and gave a national lead to students in other colleges.

Their strategy was informed by two main objectives; firstly, to build a strong anti-fascist movement, and secondly to create a revolutionary body. Two major events within days of each other in November provided the first public examples of this strategy. First, they organised a protest at the showing of *Our Fighting Navy*, a naval training information film, at The Tivoli cinema, which involved taking a seat at the cinema and shouting slogans: 'Take it off', 'We won't fight for King and country' and 'Workers unite to fight war.' A similar protest had occurred in Swindon two months earlier, resulting in arrests for breach of the peace. The Cambridge demonstration was not particularly well-organised, though four hundred students gathered outside the cinema. However they were not prepared for a counter demonstration by servicemen and right-wing students who, with the backing of a brass band, stormed onto the scene singing patriotic songs. The ensuing fracas of punches and bitter recrimination continued for weeks but was confirmation that student politics had entered public consciousness amid the wider concern over the threat of war and fascism.

Days later on Armistice Day, with feelings growing over the prospect of war, a demonstration jointly organised by the CUSS, the Student Christian movement and assorted pacifists marched through the centre of Cambridge to the War Memorial. Many students who had been horrified by the 'jingoism' and violence of the previous days came out to show their opposition to militarism. The threat of further attack and disruption by right wing students on the march was almost certainly another factor in the large numbers. Klugmann, Cornford and other communists in the CUSS were keen to avoid the demonstration being characterised as a 'student rag for poppy day' and insisted on inserting, on a large wreath, the inscription: 'To the victims of the Great War, from those who are determined to prevent similar crimes of imperialism'. (Sloan 1938) The insistence on using the word 'imperialism' prevented the participation of the League of Nations.

Police later removed the inscription on the grounds that it could lead to a breach of the peace.

The two demonstrations had helped to win more converts to the CUSS and the Party. For leading communist students, Klugmann, Cornford, Guy Burgess, Brian Simon and others, they took the battle to new heights and, along with the impact of the arrival of the Hunger Marchers the following year, were crucial in expanding the numbers of CUSS and communist influence. The Communist policy had not yet developed fully into the breadth of the Popular Front of the mid-1930s, and indeed there were sectarian moments, exemplified by a Cornford-Klugmann ill-fated intervention to counter what they saw for a while as the bourgeois influences of Auden and Spender: 'Keep Culture out of Cambridge' ('a lonely personal demonstration' as Klugmann later called it).[14]

Yet overall, the communists began to have an influence above their numbers, and Cornford and Klugmann gained a reputation for brilliant organization and as renowned recruiters and advocates who would discuss politics in student rooms long into the night. Memoirs and recollections of many who joined the Party at that time testified to their persuasive skills. Charles Rycroft, for example, distinguished their different roles by describing Klugmann as 'Mark, the 'intellectual Jesuit', and Cornford as 'Matthew, the romantic puritan'. Klugmann's own intellectual reputation was growing among his near peers, notably for his ability to articulate Marxist theory and provide a progressive reading of history, which presented communism as the only answer to depression and fascism. Victor Kiernan, later a renowned historian, regarded him as the equal of any Marxist he had encountered.

---

14   This was a title of one of Cornford's poems, the last line of which read: 'All we've brought are our Party cards, which are no bloody good for your bloody charades.' At the height of his political activity he stopped writing poetry.

A major-turning point in his rise as a communist intellectual and ultimately his decision to choose a career in the Communist Party, was the visit to Cambridge in spring 1934 of William (Willie) Gallagher, a working class leader of great prestige who would be elected as a Communist MP the following year. Gallagher was shocked by the dress, language and what he regarded as revolutionary posturing of some of the students. He told them that only a few can be full-time revolutionaries and that they should all study hard and take their academic studies seriously. The phrase 'every communist student a good student' was coined in the aftermath of this meeting. For Klugmann, it was a very profound moment and meant that he could combine his academic interests with political work. He could become a communist intellectual. As recently as October 1933, Rajani Palme Dutt, the Party's official theoretician had dismissed such a vocation.

'First and foremost he should forget he is an intellectual (except in moments of necessary self-criticism) and remember only that he is a communist.'

In the summer of 1934 Klugmann received the news that he had achieved a double first and could enrol as a research student the following year, with a fellowship firmly on the horizon.

POST-GRADUATE LIFE:
THE PROFESSIONAL COMMUNIST AND THE RME

By the end of 1934 Klugmann had already been noticed by the Party's hierarchy and had represented his student organisation at various international peace and anti-fascist congresses, notably the new Rassemblement Mondial des Etudiants (RME), the World Student Association Against War and Fascism, an international (and Comintern sponsored) gathering of left wing students, at its founding Congress. He was fluent in French and German, and now had the opportunity to spend time in France for his research under Professor Daniel Mornet at the Sorbonne. With the Party's backing and support from delegates he became part of the RME leadership from 1935 and its secretary from 1936.

His arrival in Paris, nominally to do research, but in effect to work for the Comintern – in his early days he divided his time between the Bibliothèque and the RME offices in a run-down working class suburb of Paris – coincided with big gains for the left and he witnessed massive demonstrations followed by the election of the Popular Front government. His role was to provide what would now be called 'networks' between left students across national boundaries, galvanising support for campaigns (Paris became the route for many volunteers to Spain), disseminating information, writing articles and hosting regular World Congresses. In the course of his work, he met many leading international communists and intellectuals and witnessed the workings of the Comintern at first hand. He regularly hosted his comrades from Cambridge and other British universities, who worked as volunteers or translators. These included Eric Hobsbawm, a few years behind him at Cambridge, who at the time regarded Klugmann as an intellectual guru.[15]

He also travelled extensively, notably to Yugoslavia and in 1938 to China, India and the Far East, in the company of his former Gresham's friend, Bernard Floud. The journey was significant in many ways. They had a private meeting with Mao Zedong, visited communist guerrilla groups, addressed massive gatherings in China and India, and were generally fêted as international communist leaders. The visit was also the moment when MI5 and British security services took their first serious interest in Klugmann and Floud. This was to have serious implications for their future.

---

15 Eric Hobsbawn, interview with author.

Figure 17   James Klugmann: reader's card (Photo: 'Papers of Klugmann, Marx Memorial Library and Workers' School')

The RME years were significant for Klugmann. He wrote, talked and travelled on behalf of international communism and formed the friendships and loyalties that ensured he had a career in the communist movement. The Comintern's adoption of the Popular Front in 1935 fitted perfectly into his own political outlook, and indeed endorsed much of his own thinking and practice, as his writings from that time make clear.

At the beginning of the 1930s, James Klugmann was a nervous outsider at Gresham's School, in the process of relinquishing family ties and constraints, but uncertain of what the future might hold and still in search of principles to live by. Like many others, his life was transformed by the turbulent but gripping politics of that time, which put off thoughts of an academic career, and took him from talent spotter to communist intellectual and professional revolutionary. For him and many of his comrades the revolution was close at hand and the commitment to communism was for life. His devotion to the cause would subsequently be compared to that of a 'communist Jesuit,' while the Party's allegiances and rituals reflected those of a family of sorts; he would be in the thick of the conflicts of loyalties that engulfed the Party's later years during the Cold War and its aftermath, many of which had their origins in the earlier decade.

Figure 18 Bernard Floud and James Klugmann in China, 1938 (Photo: Roderick Floud/King's College Archives, London)

Figure 19   Bernard Floud and James Klugmann meeting Mao Zedong 1938 (Photo: Roderick Floud/King's College Archives, London)

CHAPTER FOUR: MARGOT HEINEMANN

JANE BERNAL

Margot Heinemann joined the Party on the morning of October 17th 1934 when she was a post-graduate student at Newnham College, Cambridge. It is possible to be so precise about the time because it was the day the Cambridge bus strike was called off. The students who had got up early to help adjourned to a transport cafe for breakfast and Margot asked John Cornford, whom she had never met before, for a Party card (Heinemann 1986). For Margot, joining the Communist Party was not an event, more a process that had been gathering speed for the previous year. She identified two main reasons: the rise of fascism; and poverty in the UK, particularly in the Distressed Areas. Neither political theory nor the Soviet Union held any particular attraction for her. Indeed she said that she would probably have joined sooner if somebody, thinking that she was an academic kind of girl, had not asked her to read Lenin's *Materialism and Empirio-criticism* and to join a discussion group on it. She disliked and was suspicious of philosophy 'even Marxist Philosophy'. The only Marxist text she had read by the time she joined the CPGB was *State and Revolution*. When she had been in the Party for six months or so, there was an Education Class on the Communist Manifesto. The undergraduates in the Cambridge student branch were all studying for exams, so they asked Margot, who was by then a postgraduate, to be the tutor. She explained that she had never read the Manifesto. 'Now's your chance, comrade,' they told her (M. Kettle, Undated).

The Cambridge student Communist group of this period is well documented (Knox, 1989; Kiernan, 1989; Sloan, 1938; Klugmann, in Clark, 1979:13-36). The three local events that made the most impression on Margot were the Armistice Day Riots of November 1933, the arrival in Cambridge of the second Hunger March in February 1934 and the huge Anti-Fascist demonstration on September 9th 1934.

Hitler's rise to power in the spring of 1933 was however the first and most shocking event. Both Margot's parents were naturalised British citizens originating from the large German-Jewish community in Frankfurt. Her father came to England at the turn of the century, a poor relation, to take up a post in his uncle's bank. They still had family in Germany. In the UK the Tory press, particularly the *Daily Mail*, was enthusiastic about what they saw in Germany, and gave publicity to the British Union of Fascists (BUF), for example (Gardiner, 2011:435-6). *Granta*, then a weekly magazine edited by Cambridge students, carried two full page articles on *The Achievements of National Socialism*, by Dr Alwin Paul, the Hamburg Professor (1933:145). Whatever Lord Rothermere or *Granta* might think, Margot and her student friends saw Hitler's rise to power as an overwhelming international defeat. The response to the Nazis, and to Oswald Mosley's BUF in the UK, seemed feeble compared to the enormity of the threat.

'Politics was no longer just an option, a hobby – it hit you in your own life, whether you were interested or not.' (Kettle, Undated)

Before Hitler, Margot, though she had socialist views, had seen little reason to be politically active. Now she felt she had to think her way beyond the traditional pacifism and social democratic socialism that she had grown up with, to something more effective.

The Heinemann family were comfortably off, upper middle class people but 'neither rich nor smart.' Margot's parents described themselves as 'Drawing Room Socialists' and pacifists. They placed a high value on education, but do not seem to have quite understood the British school system. Margot and her older sister Dorothy went initially to the local girls high school (South Hampstead High School). Margot's poor health led to her transfer to the 'progressive' outdoor King Alfred School. Then the girls were sent to Roedean, an expensive and exclusive boarding school, where Margot developed a taste for seventeenth century poetry and a passionate loathing for philosophy and the country house life-style of her schoolmates. Initially it was Dorothy who took the greatest interest in politics. She stood as the Socialist Candidate in a school mock-election in 1929, with Margot as her agent. They gained 39 votes, out of a school of 300-odd, which was not a natural Labour constituency. Dorothy joined the Socialist Society as soon as she got to Newnham and was trained by the Labour Party in public speaking.

The disastrous 1931 General Election took place in Margot's first term at Cambridge. From that time until 1933, though she was a member of the Socialist Society, she busied herself with other things: writing, music and particularly acting. In the Lent term of 1934 she played Iras in *Antony and Cleopatra*, the first Marlowe Society production with women in female roles. She met her first serious boyfriend, David Hedley, through the drama. They joined the Party at the same time, but he went to the US on a scholarship soon after. Perhaps David cannot really be described as a middle-class recruit. A former head-boy of Eton, he was witty, charming, and strikingly good looking. He went to work full time for the Party in the US, was married twice and died relatively young, in 1948, of rheumatic heart disease.

In November 1933 Margot was involved in the Armistice Day riots. Not that she anticipated a riot. She joined what was intended to be a peaceful demonstration that was attacked by right-wing undergraduates.

The headlines in the local paper the next day were sensational. *'Battles in Cambridge Streets'*

'Truncheons Drawn by Police'
'Amazing 'Anti-War' scenes'

Of course the *Cambridge Daily News* was easily amazed, but the events of November 11th 1933 even made it into the London *Evening Standard*. Most of the demonstrators were astonished by the violence, volume and level of organisation of the opposition. They had probably been expecting a bit of heckling, but not the level of overt hostility, and not a full-blown street fight. It became part of the shared lore of the student group and appears in several memoirs and biographies (Ferry, 1998; Knox, 1998; Stansky and Abrahams, 2011; Werskey, 1978; Kiernan, 1989; Sloan, 1938).

The *Evening Standard* condemned the demonstrators, rather than their attackers, as 'hooligans':

'The behaviour of the Oxford and Cambridge undergraduates who made violent pacifist demonstrations ... is a disgrace to every member of both universities. Since the University authorities seem unable to control these young hooligans' excesses, I suggest their fellow undergraduates procure some tar. The pacifists already have the feathers.'

It made you realise, Margot said, that not everybody was in favour of peace: 'Some people are and some aren't. You had to stand up and be counted.' She wrote a piece about the affair in the Newnham student paper, *Thersites*, in the form of a Socratic dialogue between two Newnham girls (Heinemann 1933:4-6).

By January 1934 Margot was already writing home,

'This Communism business is getting more & more with us – we talk about nothing else and even Elizabeth, who has never done anything about politics, is joining a Marxist study group. Pix tends to get out of the issue by being practical & reformist, but the rest of us, including David, seem to be more or less agreed about it. Rather grim!' [16] *(Heinemann 1934)*

---

16   Elizabeth Sidgwick, later Belsey, Margot's closest Newnham friend. Pix was another friend.

Figure 20　Margot Heinemann in 1934 (Photo: Ramsey and Muspratt. By permission of Lofty Images)

When the North East coast contingent of hunger marchers arrived on February 16th 1934, students from the Socialist Society went out to meet them at Girton, on the outskirts of Cambridge, and the two groups marched into town together (Sloan 1938; Watson 2014):

'Going through town, shouting "Down with the Means Test" you would see some student you knew slightly staring, a little frightened, at the broken boots and old mackintoshes. The phrases about the power of the workers and the right to a better life suddenly meant something concrete and real.'

The meeting the next evening in the Co-op Hall in Romsey Town was addressed by Wilf Jobling, an unemployed miner from Blaydon and a Communist. Margot described his speech as a landmark, the first time that she had realised 'that the working class could have a leading role or a central role' (Heinemann 1986).

The Socialist Club and the Communist Party had worked hard to organise this event. They had held meetings and collections in all the colleges and had raised £120 – a huge sum for Cambridge at that time. There was even a debate in support of the Hunger Marchers at the Cambridge Union, the all-male student debating society. In the debate Margot's friend Jan Gillett made it clear that the essence of the Hunger March was the refusal of the unemployed to starve in silence:

'When the working class was recruited for slaughter in battle they were called heroes; when they fought for themselves, under their own leaders, they were called dupes.' (Granta.'Union Debate on Hunger March', March 7th 1934)

That, for Margot, was the crux of it.

'It was the first time I had a feeling of being part of the working class movement, and that the working classes were not people you led but were the strength, the power that was going to bring socialism about. The exploited themselves – Sklaven werden dich befreien – the slaves will set you free, the Brecht song says.' (Kettle, undated)

During that year changes were taking place in the CP, and specifically in the student Party in Cambridge, that made it more attractive to

Margot by late 1934 than it would have been in the earlier, more sectarian, Class against Class period. She was always a Popular Front Communist. She was close to her family. She was deeply interested in English Literature, particularly the drama and poetry of the Elizabethan and Jacobean period. Gallacher's call in 1934 for every Communist student to be a 'good student' made more sense to her than Dutt's 1932 requirement that a communist intellectual should 'forget that he is an intellectual and (except in moments of necessary self-criticism) remember only that he is a Communist.' (Branson 1985:122-4).

Margot gained a first class degree and a scholarship to return to Newnham for post-graduate research. That summer the BUF held a meeting at Olympia so violent that the management of the White City cancelled their booking for a further rally in September. The BUF called a meeting in Hyde Park instead.

'Drown the Blackshirts in a Sea of Working-class Activity' was, Margot reflected in the 1980s, a rather curious slogan, not just because it was dated, but because it is in that peculiar language which she called Runglish (English with Russian phraseology). For all that, it described the event pretty accurately. Down on the ground Margot was aware that she and her friends from King's were part of a vast crowd, who were indeed mainly workers, filling Hyde Park and neighbouring streets. There were no loudspeakers and any banners were furled as each group entered the park. From where she was she could not see the fascists raising their right arms in the 'Hitler Salute', or the ring of police who surrounded them. It is clearer in photographs taken from a height, that were shown in the *Illustrated London News*, and are still available via the internet (http://longstreet.typepad.com/thesciencebookstore/2013/03/crowd-series.html). At the centre are about 2,000 Blackshirts including Sir Oswald Mosley himself, wearing smart military style uniforms; then come 6,000 police, mounted and on foot, and the surrounding anti-fascists who numbered at least 100,000, perhaps as many as 150,000.

The turnout was the more remarkable because the TUC and the Labour Party had advised people to stay away.

It was that demonstration, Margot said, that made her finally decide to join the Communist Party. It was clear to her that the communists were prepared to take on the fascists, and that the communists knew how to organise a mass movement. It was her experience of political activity that led to a decision that was neither impulsive nor particularly romantic.

CHAPTER FIVE: LEN JONES

PHILIP COHEN

My uncle Len Jones was a self-made intellectual who started life in a poor working-class home in Liverpool. Through brilliant academic work he won a scholarship first to the Liverpool Institute then to Cambridge University's Christ's College to study Greek and Latin, even winning the Porson Prize in his second year for translating a passage of English poetry into Greek iambic verse. It was at Cambridge that he joined the Communist Party in 1934. He gained a reputation as a hardliner and much later, in 1961, frustrated with his job as a school teacher and disillusioned with the CPGB, moved with his family to work in the German Democratic Republic as a university lecturer and translator, living there until his death in 2003. It is worth noting in passing that he was the only Jewish boy at the Institute, and was therefore kept out of morning prayers and from the weekly religious instruction lesson. Some of the boys made fun of him for this and even threatened him physically. Whether this 'outsider' status led him more readily to embrace the CPGB is hard to say.

He certainly didn't have a political upbringing. He was born in London's East End in 1913; his father was first a coppersmith then a travelling salesman, and also a tenor who sang in travelling opera companies and the local synagogue. His mother was a buttonhole maker. Her parents were recent Jewish immigrants from Lithuania. Len's family moved to Liverpool and lived in some rooms behind and above a watchmaker's shop in what he called 'a semi-slum' without a hot water system. In his memoir, *Pages from the Life of a Teacher* (Jones

1998), Len says his mother never read a book or newspaper and was ignorant of the world outside. Though he was very attached to him – he took him to concerts and the opera – his father was conservative in outlook, voted Tory, and was a reader of the 'reactionary, yellow press', such as the *News of the World* and *Titbits*. What he describes as 'the most shattering experience of my life' occurred in February 1934 when, following frequent rows with his wife, his father left the family home and four children, including my mother Eve, to live with another woman. They never saw him again. The family were left literally penniless and only survived because of financial help from the Jewish Board of Guardians.

Len joined the CPGB just nine months later in his third year at Cambridge, but it is difficult to know whether this family trauma played a part and if his decision was some sort of reaction against it. In any case there were other forces at play, as Nicholas Deakin has pointed out: rapidly rising unemployment, Oswald Mosley's fascist party, and the CPGB's embrace of the new 1934-5 Comintern line to build Popular Fronts and welcome members from a variety of backgrounds.

Len, given his original working-class origins, was certainly perfect recruit material. He describes how two fellow students who were Communists invited him to meetings of the Socialist Society, where he heard speeches by Shapurgi Saklatvala, a former Communist MP endorsed by the Labour Party; Ernst Toller, a left-wing German playwright; and most memorably Harry Pollitt, General Secretary of the CPGB. Pollitt spoke to a packed meeting at the Guildhall. 'When question time came one student called out, 'What is the difference between Stalin and Mae West?' Harry said, 'If that is the best you can do, it's a great pity about all that money your parents have spent on your education.' This was well received by the students, who no doubt felt guilty about their privileged upbringing in the midst of the depression and mass unemployment. His friends got Len to read the Saturday issue

Figure 21   Len, Barbara and Eve Jones (later Cohen). (Photo: the author)

of the *Daily Worker*, and he then joined the 300-strong student branch of the CPGB led by historian and poet John Cornford. He bought a copy of Engels' *'Anti-Dühring*,' and says he learnt a lot from it.

It was clashes with Mosley's fascists that he remembered most vividly and which seemed to have brought the greatest excitement. In one, Len helped to stop an open-air meeting in Cambridge addressed by Alexander Raven Thomson, Oswald Mosley's Director of Policy. A large group of Communist students infiltrated the audience on parkland in front of the speaker, who was standing on the roof of a van, and started heckling. In the end Raven Thomson had to give up and drive away. 'My friend and comrade Elia had come with a quire of *Daily Workers* to sell,' Len said. 'All of a sudden a young man who must have been a Fascist jumped at Elia and tried to snatch the papers from him. I also took a jump and beat him off. He was of a type characteristic of Mosley's Fascism – brutal and cowardly.' Soon after this there was another clash when about 50 students cycled to Saffron Walden where Raven Thomson was due to speak again. 'Led by James Klugmann the students heckled the speaker throughout all his attempts to speak and he finally gave up and disappeared,' Len said.

I asked my uncle once whether he knew any of the Cambridge spies like Philby and Burgess and he, perhaps understandably, changed the subject. They do seem to have been at Cambridge earlier than Len so it is possible he didn't meet them, but he certainly appears to have known James Klugmann (see essay by Geoff Andrews, above) and mixed in the CPGB circles until he left the university.

I remember him as a contradictory figure, possessing a lively mind, fond of folk and classical music, chess and bridge, theatre and opera, happy to discuss the football results, yet also a rigid Communist who seemed to find a purpose and vocation in CPGB Party work and adopted Marxist theory as a guide to his own life. One of his heroes was the Russian Bolshevik teacher and writer Anton Makarenko who

Figure 22   Len Jones, 1930s (Photo: the author)

describes in his book, *Road to Life* (1955), how he sought to re-educate difficult children, which led them to buckle down and co-operate.

Len was impressed with this, and relates a later incident about his relationship with his stepson Achim, the child of his German wife Kaethe, whom he met during the war and subsequently married in Liverpool. One day he caught Achim and his friends throwing stones and told him he must stop it.

'The next day I came home from school – only to see Achim throwing stones again! I gave him one smack in the face. This use of physical force would be condemned as bourgeois cruelty by libertarian parents, but I hold it with Makarenko, who clouted one of his children's group for outrageous conduct against the welfare of his fellow human beings. Had I not done what I considered to be my duty, serious consequences could easily have followed. Achim threw no more stones.'

One of his sons, Martin Jones, interviewed in my book *Children of the Revolution* (Cohen 1997), referred to this tendency of his father to follow Soviet teaching and the Moscow line in everything.

'He was not a Communist; he was really a Stalinist; that was my opinion. Anything about the purges and what Stalin did was propaganda, it never happened. There must have been a few reasons for the camps, the Gulags, but I never spoke about it, I didn't dare. He never said how he got into politics, just that his family was very, very poor, he loved his father, and his father left the family, and he had to take care of the family. He was very fond of his sister, Eve [see essay by Norma Cohen, below], and he had to raise money for the family. He did a good job in that and saved the family probably. My father had a very good brain in his subject, but he was absolutely disabled in tackling things in normal life.'

CHAPTER SIX: EVE AND ERIC COHEN

NORMA COHEN

For my parents Eve and Eric Cohen, the Communist Party provided an alternative paradigm, a new 'family of man' they could both embrace, with its unswerving sense of purpose, its cultural activities and comradeship coupled with a gut response to the Depression years and a worship of all things Soviet with its unsullied vision of equality for all. They both stayed on to the end, a lifelong commitment which sailed through traumatic change. My brother Maurice suggests it was a love affair in which judgment and facts were suspended.

As my father put it: 'Marxism is a bit like a drug. Once it's in your body, it stays there.' A declassé Marxist intellectual who became Chief Accountant for the *Morning Star* from 1961 into the `80s, his early, lifelong conversion transmuted in his late eighties into quietly campaigning for the Labour Party.

Eric was born in Liverpool in 1912 to Jewish emigré parents who had fled Russia in 1905; his father Label a bespoke tailor, his mother Gitel a peasant grocer's daughter who educated herself to read Tolstoy and Dickens in English, reputedly marched with the Suffragettes along Lime Street and poured her zeal into Zionism.

Repeatedly expelled from grammar schools for truancy and bad behaviour, he was a born anarchist with an insouciant attitude towards authority. A slightly built if hardy boy, constitutionally incapable of street gang warfare, he became an idealist with a fierce sense of morality. His mission, like that of the prankster *Till Eulenspiegel*, the Robin Hood of German folklore, was to sidestep authority, outwit bullies and expose wrongdoing. With the clear eyes and quick wit of an eternal child, he never really grew up. Like Jessica Mitford's description of husband Esmond Romilly, Eric seemed to have been born without the slightest sense of dealing with the physical world around him. 'One had the feeling that he had never even really learnt to tie his shoes.'

But his enlightened music master Wallace – Eric's 'Jean Brodie' of the 1920s – took his charges to gallery seats at the Liverpool Playhouse, where the radical visions of Sean O'Casey, Brecht and Shakespeare melded with Browning, Robert Louis Stevenson and later Heine to fire Eric's idealistic spirit with a fierce sense of morality, their every line redolent of adventure, danger and escape.

Five young cousins from 'the distinguished emigré branch of the family on Father's side, all great readers with a working class outlook', had themselves turned to the Communist Party, and were active in the swiftly growing solidarity movement, The International Association of Friends of the Soviet Union.

Their stand made perfect sense to my father. In the `20s and `30s Depression years, the family had witnessed the hunger marches through Liverpool. He became angry at the folly of the capitalist system that rendered people jobless and destitute overnight. A punitive Versailles treaty decimated German currency in the wake of World War I. He'd seen his father wave around a note for fifty million Marks donated by a grateful customer. Worthless, cried Label, not even enough to buy a loaf of bread. Up and down the country, agitators were having buckets of water — the equivalent of today's water cannons — thrown over their heads by the police. The popular climate was unstable. People were eager for change. It said so in the cooperative paper *Reynolds News*.

An active dreamer, he saw himself on the brink of a changing world as a humanist, cosmopolitan and internationalist. He'd seen his parents occasionally at breaking point, dodging bailiffs at the door and struggling to remake themselves. Now, with his passion for justice

Figure 23   Eric Cohen (Photo: the author)

and fair play, and in his rejection of every recognised order he'd so far met, there was a chance to make a difference in society, to dedicate his energy to something worthwhile. A man on a mission, intent on changing the world.

Aged sixteen, after a brief spell as a practising vegetarian, an indigestible stand to adopt in a kosher chicken-focused household like his mother Gitel's, he became secretary of the flourishing YCL (Young Communist League) and Friends of the Soviet Union. Following his mother's example, he embraced Marxism through self-education, reading Ralph Fox's biography of Lenin, with Russia as the model for the future development of modern societies.

Regarded by the rest of his family as a shadowy figure, he allegedly set up home in the attic. In his upturning of every occasional Jewish table, Eric clashed with his intimidating, entrepreneurial father, when he was forced to work for him if jobs were hard to come by. But perhaps he nevertheless inherited the seeds of his anti-establishment stand from Label, who had himself mixed with an anarchist crowd back in the *haim* (homeland) and had mythically been a member of the Jewish secular union, the Bund: 'organise educate agitate' in Yiddish, the language of the masses, which had played its own part in the formation of the Russian Communist Party.

Eric shunned his parents' aspirational need to conform; their attempts to upgrade their status from small time *stetl* shopkeepers scrabbling a living at the shabby end of Liverpool to genteel, petit bourgeois, Anglo-Jewry professionals, with a nod to the King. The five sons were called by classic English names. His four brothers were all more conformist and Jewish observant. They embraced comfortable respectability as solicitors, chemist and accountant, moving into positions of professional responsibility from which Eric would shy away. He alone rebelled, adopting a value system that embodied all the restless, wayward qualities. Why? Perhaps he did it for them.

He longed to plunge into covert, antifascist activity, joining the Communist Party in the 1930s when pro-Mosley rallies in the centre of Liverpool inevitably ended in beatings. As a twenty five year old in 1938, Eric heard that his literary hero Ralph Fox – newly enlisted in the International Brigades to fight for the Spanish Republic – had just been killed in the battle of Lopera. Fearless and selfless, he'd willingly have joined veteran Liverpool comrade Jack Coward, a seadog warrior and 'a fine CP-er', who'd written of his adventures infiltrating Franco's battle lines at Teruel in *Back from the Dead*, a book my father treasured. He turned up to enlist at Party HQ in Picton Road, but was rejected, bitterly disappointed, in favour of the growing band of unemployed workers and younger unmarried men.

Socialist publisher Victor Gollancz's newly established Left Book Club, a fast-growing clearing house with discussion groups and newsletters sounding the key clarion call against fascism, offered cut-price editions like *Spain in Revolt* and Stafford Cripps' *Struggle for Peace*. Elected onto a committee with top Merseyside union leader Leon McGree, Eric eagerly looked forward to all the bureaucratic activities comrades were supposed to take part in, but discovered his meagre function as a one man Party literature stall was to sell books to contacts in the Jewish community, 'such as they were'. For my father, this was a lousy assignation.

As an unwilling junior clerk in a firm of chartered accountants, he became member of a string of progressive organisations, including the Clerk's Union, adopting the Communist Party view of the trades councils as models of how socialism could develop in Britain as mini Soviets.

His casual dismissal of 'the Trots' (Trotskyists), labeled 'a band of snuffling pigs' by the British Communist Party, revealed conflicted feelings about his own middle class origins. Longing to be a man of the people with a cloth cap and accent to match, he would forever call people 'Chief'.

Figure 24 Eric Cohen on a demonstration (Photo: the author)

Our mother Eve's involvement was emotional. The Party gave her the opportunity to escape her impoverished background. It offered her a raison d'être, a way of realising herself, transcending the constrictions of her working class background. Via Eric, she could embrace a second family, this one open-armed and Jewish.

She was born in 1919 near the Liverpool docks to an errant 'fancy goods' commercial traveller father with a passion for light opera, who was a member of the Carl Rosa Opera and musical director of the Liverpool Jewish Choir. There was no money for books, clothes or entertainment. One book, *The Poor Cow*, was passed around among the four children. At twelve, she won a scholarship to a church school, but without a decent pair of shoes, she had to wait until 1932 when her absent father sent ten shillings: 'My ticket to education'. Against the odds, she made it to grammar school but was forced to jettison her Matric to get out and earn a living aged seventeen, in order to support the family by working in a jeweller's. Drear and deprivation characterised by eviction, bailiffs and occasional handouts from the Jewish Board of Guardians made her hungry for change.

Christmas 1939, and she was twenty. Reeling off into the blackout, she arrived at an imposing house and knocked on a door that opened with a blast of hot air to change her life. There was her brother Len, her sister Barbara and fifty other teenagers who gravitated towards the Young Communist League to sing *The Red Flag* and *Bandiera Rossa*, a revolutionary rallying song popularised during the Spanish Civil War.

A fellow called Eric had watched her walk in with her curly black hair and round cheeks, reminding him of his own Communist cousin, Una. Whilst succumbing to the deviationist, bourgeois cult of the individual was not on his agenda, he asked her to dance. 'Quickstep's not my strong point', he apologised, stepping on her toes for the umpteenth time. 'And what is?' enquired Eve, as the Dashing White Sergeant started up. 'Oh, debating, crosswords, chess, classical music, politics, Esperanto is the new international language. I've been studying it on a storm course. If everyone in the world had the same common language, there'd be no more wars or misunderstandings, or so the theory goes.' 'Oh.' 'And as you know, theory and practice are two very different things. Life's a bundle of contradictions.'

That was enough for my mother, the game of ghosts and the folk dancing. Now she had a mission. Though the snow was waist high, she walked a couple of hours from Abacus Road to Lime Street station to collect bulk orders of *Challenge*, the YCL's campaigning newspaper, from the London train. She heaved her mammoth bundles of quires onto the creaking steps of a tram. 'Upstairs only!' shouted the conductor, shoving her up.

Eric invited Eve to hike round Snowdon with him on the YCL's regular North Wales beat. It was their second date. Struggling up Glydder Pass, he instructed her, 'I'll carry the pots and pans and you carry the selected works of Lenin in your rucksack.'

Those books were so heavy, I had to walk bent double all the way. The people going from hostel to hostel christened me the bloodhound, because my nose was so close to the ground. Then he dropped his own rucksack, so all the pots and pans went clattering down the cliff.'

In the fifties, she'd be trained as a public speaker by 'our beloved top comrade Harry Pollitt', in charge of political work amongst women and fundraiser extraordinaire. At only four foot eleven, she was a dead ringer for Dolores, 'La Pasionaria', the Spanish Civil War's Rosa Luxemburg. You have to be a tiny woman to be a legend. She rose to serve on the District Committee (DC), then the Executive Committee (EC), regarded as giving selfless, unflinching devotion and tireless loyalty to family and comrades alike.

Later she'd enrol on a mature students' teacher training course and write her thesis on the legacy of Elizabeth Garrett Anderson and the Suffragettes.

Figure 25 Eve Cohen (née Jones) (Photo: the author)

The Communist Party gave her an outlet for her intelligence and an outlook on life she couldn't find anywhere else – feeling at one with vast humanity – an alternative home and safe haven. It was also a way of transcending present deprivations with a shining belief in the future, a vision of a new world. Things could only get better. The Party completed the education she'd been pulled away from, with its emphasis on ideas, reading and personal development, a belief her situation could be changed by structure and discipline.

Like Esmond Romilly's category of real communists:

'To fit in, you had to be a serious person, a rigid disciplinarian, interested in all the technical aspects of warfare, lacking in any such selfish motive as fear or reckless courage.'

Campaigning for change seems to have been the basis of the lifelong project both our parents were engaged in, with its puritan emphasis on austerity and stern discipline of mind over matter, putting the Party's needs first in all aspects of their lives.

They extolled the Communist Party dictum of family sacrifice for the greater good: socialism and communism first, domestic life second. My father carted along Party literature even on his wedding day in 1940, when he informed his wife to be: 'I dedicate my life to the Communist Party and whatever's left you're welcome to.' This assertion of the political over the personal meant his abdicating responsibility for child rearing and domestic work and, as a political activist, being a virtually absent father for most of our childhood.

But both my parents embraced the pull of consuming tasks and commitments without questioning the correctness of the Party line. They were happy to serve on committees and campaigned as Communist candidates in the local elections. There was always something to do to lend life extra meaning. Making themselves useful was the highest goal.

Figure 26   Eric and Eve Cohen, 1940 (Photo: the author)

CHAPTER SEVEN: JAMES MACGIBBON

HAMISH MACGIBBON

My father, James MacGibbon, was born 1912 into a wealthy Scottish family; his father was minister of Glasgow Cathedral, Church of Scotland; his mother had inherited a fortune from her father's shipping business. James was educated at Fettes College, the English public school in Edinburgh (an experience which reinforced his scepticism for authority). On leaving school at the age of 17, he was employed by a publisher who later allowed him a sabbatical to live with an aristocratic, cultured Prussian family in Berlin, where for 18 months he worked for a printer, and became fluent in German. The contrast between the Weimar world of art and literature in which he became immersed, and bourgeois Scotland, was a life-long influence. Politically naïve as he was, he was disturbed by what was going on in Germany in 1933 – and could hardly fail to be so (he encountered a Jewish publisher in tears, his books taken for burning). In 1935 he married my mother, Jean, who had been raised in a comfortably off family – her father was a partner in a firm of accountants – and had been educated at St Leonard's Girls' School. Settling in London that year they went to the Conservative Party ball at the Albert Hall. But they also became acquainted with radical artists and journalists (my mother was a budding writer). A year later, James overheard in a pub someone praising Francoists for their 'war on Communist scum' in Spain, stirring in him the beginnings of political awakening.

Figure 27   James MacGibbon, 1932 (Photo: the author)

My parents became involved in setting up (with the left-wing vicar of Putney Parish Church, Stephan Hopkinson) a home for Basque children refugees and, approaching Liberal and Labour parties for help, were told, 'We mustn't jeopardise Britain's commitment to non-intervention'. However, the local Communist Party offered practical support without hesitation. So my parents decided to join. Talking with like-minded people, they understood that at stake was not only the baleful impact of the Nationalist invasion on ordinary people and the democratic government of Spain – powerful enough motivation in itself – but also the future of Europe as a whole. Like many others, Churchill included, they foresaw that if the forces of Germany and Italy were successful in Spain while France and Britain and other democratic countries stood aside, it would be an open door to domination of Europe. It was clear to many (Churchill not included!) that the Communists were the one Party taking an effective and unequivocal anti-Fascist stance. At the same time my parents, as they became more politically educated, grasped the relevance of Marxist ideas to the condition of Britain: the collapse of the economy, chronic unemployment and poverty, and the inability and lack of will of establishment parties to find any significant remedies. James remembered how as a child he was required on one or two occasions to accompany his father on parochial visits to slum dwellings in Glasgow. Riding in his father's car through the Gorbals in winter he saw children with bare feet.

In the Party my parents made lasting friendships with working-class people whom they would otherwise have not got to know well. When they applied to join, James and Jean were visited by the secretary of the Barnes branch, Pat Paterson. His wife Margaret had an eight-month old baby, the same age as my mother's first (me), and they became friends. Jean wrote about Margaret's family:

'The Elmses were a remarkable lot, and my time in the Barnes CP would have been a lot duller without them. At least three of them would have qualified today to go to university. As it was, those three, including Margaret, died of TB. The Elmses used to tease us about idealising "the workers" after the fashion of middle-class comrades: "the workers – the sods! They're no better than anyone else!" Our friendship with the family was lasting.' (MacGibbon, 1984)

With the termination of the Party's 'class against class' phase in favour of the Popular Front, members had been encouraged to become involved in a range of liberal-minded movements. University students were urged to make the most of their courses so that they could make a Marxist contribution to the sciences and arts (and, for the group of secret members recruited by the NKVD, would rise to influential positions in the Foreign Office and intelligence services). Political activity was thus enlivened for James by his association with the Artists' International Association (AIA), a left-wing group of, mostly, painters and designers. Misha Black, one of the leading designers of the time, was chairman. At an AIA dance James and Jean danced under a gigantic Alexander Calder mobile. Membership included many leading artists such as Henry Moore and my parents' newly acquired friend, the painter Julian Trevelyan.

Following Pat Paterson, James became secretary of the Barnes Party. With his social style and fine speaking voice, inherited from his father, he was a welcome upper middle-class recruit. His public speaking was enhanced by tuition from a Party expert (he used the method of writing key points on cards, thus acquired, for his many speeches for the rest of his life). Jean combined political activism with bringing up two young children. One of her chores was delivering the *Daily Worker*, with a pram carrying bundles of the paper along with my sister Janet and me. James was frequently out in the evenings at political and social meetings. Jean involved herself with the Co-op Guild, often taking members in their Morris station wagon to meetings. On one hugely popular May Day march I, at the age of three, was dressed in Spanish Republican Army uniform, standing with my mother on a platform on my parents' station-wagon roof, when we joined the procession to Hyde Park. And there we met James and Jean's friend, young and pretty Jocelyn Herbert (who became a leading London theatre designer) wearing a garden-party hat, along with her solicitor husband Anthony Lousada, though he was no Communist. James, looking back on those heady days, thought,

'It was the feeling that we were part of a movement that would change the world that kept us going. It was for people like us a time of political innocence: we believed that the Soviet Union would lead us to a new, enlightened age and it must be supported.'

On Britain's declaration of war with Germany, James volunteered for an infantry regiment and was commissioned in the Royal Fusiliers. As a Communist he was contravening the Party line at that time – because of the Molotov-Ribbentrop pact the conflict was deemed a 'Capitalist War' – and he resigned from the Party. All the same he and his wife maintained their political attachment and they rejoined after the German invasion of the Soviet Union.

As it happened, because of his fluent German, James was transferred to the Military Intelligence Corps. In spring 1941, he was posted to MO3 (Military Operations Section 3) in the War Office, that dealt with plans for 'Overlord,' the code name for the invasion of France – an objective that seemed all too distant in those grim early days.

Then Hitler invaded the USSR, and at last Britain was not alone. Winston Churchill broadcast that, 'The Russian danger is our danger … just as the cause of any Russian fighting for his hearth and home is the cause of free men and free peoples in every corner of the globe.' It was a short time after the Battle of Moscow, probably in early spring 1942, that James became directly involved in the war on the Eastern

Front. When he was on night duty he sat in the War Office room where the positions of enemy and allied forces worldwide were shown on a huge map. The Military Operations and Military Intelligence sections met for regular coffee breaks where, after June 1941, the situation in Russia was the main topic of discussion. James was outraged that we were not doing everything we could to help our ally, at that time the only country to be waging all-out war against the Germans at the cost of massive loss of life day by day. Through a mutual friend with left-wing sympathies, James was put in touch with someone from the Soviet Embassy, presumably a GRU (Soviet Army Intelligence) agent. The Russian officer confirmed that the British were not communicating important intelligence about their mutual enemy, Nazi Germany.

The most important instance in which James passed information was Kursk, the greatest tank battle in history. In the six months following the Stalingrad surrender, the Germans fought several defensive battles in the spring of 1943, at first gradually giving way under Soviet pressure, though at the expense of considerable Russian losses in men and equipment. Then the Germans gathered their strength for an ambitious attempt to encircle and destroy a large part of the Soviet front line troops – tactics they had successfully pursued in previous campaigns. But by now the Russian armies were well prepared, in the number and quality of tanks, anti-tank guns and other weaponry, air cover and, as well as skilful tactics and not least, experienced commanders and other ranks, battle-hardened over the previous two years. In contrast to earlier battles, they also possessed excellent information about German dispositions. Some of this came from John Cairncross, who passed on 'raw' intelligence from Bletchley Park code-breaking centre. James MacGibbon seems to have been another contributor.

It should be made clear that James's wartime espionage had no resemblance to the treasonous activities of Philby and others who sent highly damaging information to the Soviet Union during the Cold War, which also led to the deaths of many of our agents in Eastern Europe. Whereas the 'Cambridge Five' were moles, recruited in the 1930s and remaining under cover, James was open about his former membership of the Party. He was a patriot whose sole concern was to assist our ally (and thus the Allies as a whole) in the War. He almost certainly made a significant contribution to the Soviet Union's desperate battle for survival and then to an extraordinary victory, won at the cost of about 25 million lives.

After the War ended James and Jean were active Party members. James was appointed secretary of the committee responsible for organising the pageant at the Albert Hall in 1948 to celebrate the centenary of the Communist Manifesto. During the 1950s Jean became increasingly disillusioned with the Party and joined the Labour Party. James followed her in 1956, soon after Khrushchev's 20th Party Congress revelations. They remained Labour and CND activists for the rest of their lives. James died in 2000 and Jean in 2002.

CHAPTER EIGHT: MARY MCINTOSH AND RICHARD CLARK

ELIZABETH DOLAN

My parents' Communism was the catalyst for the family discussions which led to my interest and involvement in this project. Our conversations were prompted by the desire expressed by my uncle, Ronald McIntosh, to pay tribute to his sister (my mother), and by extension to my father. Mary McIntosh and Richard Clark were not the sort of people one would have heard of in the ordinary course of events. Yet they exemplify the later careers of a considerable number of those middle-class recruits caught up in the heady enthusiasm of the 1930s who did not go on to be household names but whose idealism endured. At the time of course there was no particular reason to suppose that some were headed for relative obscurity, or that others were likely to become better known. To a considerable extent that must have been the luck of the draw, as well as individual choices about post-university occupation and residence, but equally a result of the need or lack of need for paid employment. Wartime roles must also have had an impact. After the war many will have found their links with former friends and associates loosened, even perhaps completely severed.

That Communist episode, intellectual and idealistic though it may have been, certainly coloured and underpinned my parents' later working and social lives. They shared many formative experiences with their contemporaries, and, like others, they were the product of their background and environment. However, their characters were formed as much because of, rather than in spite of the specific attributes of their own parents and the family life they created, circumstances which were perhaps as influential as any external factors could be. Unlike those of their contemporaries who discarded their ideals, often quite publicly, and were considered turncoats or renegades, Mary and Richard built on this epoch in their lives in an extraordinarily creative way.

My parents, Richard Clark (1915-88) and Mary McIntosh (1916-2005), grew up in London in comfortable, cultured and affectionate families. Both families were, and always remained, very supportive and although the parents may not always have sympathised with the activities and beliefs of their offspring, they were sufficiently broadminded for there never to have been any hint of estrangement. So it was with the background of this familial security that Richard and Mary were able to experiment with the process of growing up and making their own way in the world. It was in that secure childhood that they first encountered so many of the things that were ultimately to shape their lives.

My mother's father was a doctor, a GP before the war and subsequently Medical Officer of Health in Hendon who was then seconded as a civil servant to the Ministry of Health in the mid-1930s; my father's father, though largely a self-made man, rose to be a company secretary working in the City of London, who was able to send his sons to public school and university and to live in considerable material comfort. In both cases, specific artistic influence came from the maternal side: my mother's mother spent a year in Paris, living with a family and studying singing, later performing at subscription concerts and in private houses in and around Edinburgh before her marriage in 1912; my father's mother had acquired a reasonable proficiency in drawing as a young woman (she had been a pupil-teacher) and encouraged my father's early efforts in that line.

Both families belonged to that sector of the middle class which had to work for a living, and my father believed firmly throughout his life that capital, however accumulated (and both my grandfathers had invested shrewdly), was held in trust for the benefit of all humanity, and was not a private luxury to be squandered. As I remember my father's view, capital could be harnessed as the servant of communist ideals and used for purposes of research and investment in the infrastructure of manufacturing. I am not sure he ever finally reconciled the two systems in his mind or his practice, but his working life was a continuous striving towards that goal.

Both Richard and Mary attended public schools as day pupils, Richard as a King's Scholar at Westminster, and Mary at South Hampstead High School. Both schools seem to have had a fairly relaxed attitude to the extent to which pupils were exposed to progressive thinking, both social and overtly political. The fact of being day pupils is significant because of the contrast it makes with the experience of so many children of the middle class who were automatically sent as boarders to both prep and public schools. Boarding meant a divided life, rather than an intermingled one; school and home could be considered as unrelated worlds, existing in their own compartments. As day pupils living all the time at home, however, people like my parents will have encountered a wide diversity of attitudes and ideas both within and outside the family circle, for example in the homes of their friends, thus exposing them to differing opinions about current events, both political and cultural.

While boarding schools of course had a range of societies and clubs, the membership of these would come from the same confined world of the particular school. Day pupils in similar organisations on the other hand could mingle with young people (and often adults) from other backgrounds and with other lifestyles. This would also be true of political groupings; although it has been suggested that communist cells existed in a number of public schools, to be involved in a communist branch with no connection to a school would be a very different experience and would expose school-aged members to more wide-ranging activity. There is no evidence that my parents were involved in such activity, but it cannot be ruled out as a possibility.

In their daily journeys through London my parents will have been aware of the social and economic inequality around them: working class hardship, unemployment and poverty were sufficiently widespread and visible on the streets. They may have been aware of and possibly actually witnessed hunger marches and rallies. And for anything they did not see at first hand, there were enough harrowing descriptions in the novels and factual accounts of the 19th and early 20th centuries, as well as, increasingly, post-revolutionary works about the theory and practice of communism, to fuel a nascent sense of the injustices of life and a way to remove them. Both my parents were avid readers and collectors of books, and always attached great importance to their power as propaganda and as an educational tool.

As a post-war Europe became more readily accessible for holiday travel, horizons widened and people could see for themselves what life was like across the Channel: Europe became perhaps more significant than the Empire for the younger generation. This was particularly the case for Mary, who used to talk of the whole family taking off with the car for six weeks in the summer, travelling through France and to Austria, for example. Richard's family tended to holiday in the West Country, but his father had travelled to Siberia and British Columbia as a young man. Additionally, there were family connections on his mother's side with Egypt and Australia. So for Richard the lure of far distant places was well-entrenched by the time he went up to Oxford and he then took advantage of various possibilities for travel – with college friends to Greece (through Yugoslavia and on a cruise), to France to take part in an archaeological dig and later with Mary's family.

Both travelled independently to Germany in their late teens – my father to Heidelberg in 1933 and my mother to Hamburg in 1934 where she spent five months living with a family and studying German (a replication of her own mother's experience). The rather sketchy descriptions and comments that both let fall when we were children suggest that what they experienced chimed in closely with accounts given in memoirs and novels of the times. (One of my father's photographs is of the notorious *Juden sind hier nicht erwünscht* sign, which many others have recalled seeing throughout Germany in the thirties.) They will have been able to see for themselves the early developments of the fascist aspects of Nazism following Hitler's rise to power, and may perhaps have had a glimpse of student Communism.

Feminism, anti-fascism, and pacifism have all been cited as elements in the soup of influences on this generation, and my parents will not have been immune to them.

My mother was quintessentially a feminist (in the circumscribed terms of the day) as well as an egalitarian: the books she herself read in those impressionable teenage years and those she recommended to us reflected a growing independence and autonomy for women. I suspect that the germs of this lay in her own mother's life, whose youthful independence was a source of anecdotes told with relish to her grand-daughters. Mary herself insisted on her right to a university education, in emulation of an older cousin.

Like the others within this group, my parents grew up in the shadow of the Great War and there can be no doubt that this too was a strong influence. My mother's father served in the RAMC (in a base hospital near Boulogne) and although his children were shielded from the horrors he had seen, they will have been in no doubt about his feelings that war was a terrible thing and should never happen again. Both my parents developed strong pacifist views, campaigning as undergraduates for the Youth Peace Assembly, and yet they saw no alternative to war in the struggle against fascism, both in Spain and against the Nazis – Hitler had to be defeated. British politics in the 1930s, both domestic

Figure 28   An anti-Jewish sign in Germany, 1933 (Photo: Richard Clark)

and foreign, seemed inept and blinkered. The overt support for fascism, and the governing classes' arrogant disregard for the less advantaged will have reinforced the idea that Communism held the key to the future.

For my father, there was another quite potent influence at work and that was the romantic version of Russia culled from his own father's experiences as a young man, which seems to have exerted a powerful magnetism on his imagination. Shortly before the War, Richard's father's business connections led to his becoming part of a syndicate to exploit a copper mine in pre-revolutionary Kazakhstan. He was appointed Company Secretary and travelled to Russia in about 1912 on a tour of inspection. (As a man of twenty, he had earlier been sent to British Columbia for similar reasons.) No doubt he returned from these expeditions with a fund of traveller's tales for the later fascination of his children. Throughout his life, Richard retained a keen interest in the writings of Russian authors from Tolstoy and the memoirs of Aksakov via orthodox Soviet novelists to the much later dissident writings of Solzhenitsyn and others.

No single one of these factors will necessarily have triggered an instant conversion, but collectively, they will undoubtedly have opened my parents' minds to the political world and contributed to the gradual development of a philosophy of life and a political creed from their teenage years onwards. (Philosophy was an important element in their subsequent university degree courses – for my father Classical Mods and Greats and for my mother PPE – which will have helped them to be clear-minded about their beliefs, perhaps embedding those all the more firmly.)

Their Oxford careers came plumb in the middle of the period we are considering: Richard at Christ Church (1934-38) and Mary at St. Hugh's (1935-38). Here their earlier political interests blossomed into a much fuller involvement. It is likely that the focus of their political involvement was in 1936-37, tailing off in 1938 perhaps in deference

Figure 29   Mary McIntosh (Photo: the author)

Figure 30   Richard Clark (Photo: the author)

to examination pressures; although my father described himself as a 'student in my spare time', and certainly they had multiple non-academic calls on their energies, both were able and conscientious students who could have expected better results than they actually achieved. They were both active in the Oxford University Labour Club: others have indicated that during this period the OULC was thoroughly infiltrated by the Communists among the undergraduates. They wrote for its *Bulletin* (in some of whose articles there is overt Communism), as did some who later became very well known, and from internal evidence – stylistic as well as specific comments – I think it is probable that my father was for a time involved in the editing of the journal. They took part in campaigning – in local elections in Oxford, where Communists joined forces with Labour to ensure an electoral gain; they went on demonstrations – in London against Oswald Mosley and even, one of my sisters recalls being told, travelling to Paris to march with their student counterparts against Hitler. They were involved in movements such as the Youth Peace Campaign, and attended summer camps in Kent and possibly the Welsh Marches. Although our evidence is fragmentary and mostly circumstantial, some of it is to my mind fairly conclusive and it is my uncle's firm belief, from conversations with his sister Mary at the time, that they were in a formal sense members of the CPGB.

One of Richard's many interests while at Oxford was archaeology, to which he was heavily committed during several vacations, digging as a student under Sir Mortimer Wheeler and his wife Tessa Verney, notably at Maiden Castle and in Brittany. He obviously achieved a degree of responsibility (e.g. report writing) and seems to have been well regarded. He had an ambition to bring his interest in archaeology and in Russia/Communism together in a research project to investigate the Roman influence in the Pontic region around the Black Sea and in the Caucasus, for which he proposed learning Russian so that he could make use of libraries in Leningrad. This is another instance in which early influences and student preoccupations come together to shape future lives. There is also an echo of his father's connection with Kazakhstan. Unfortunately for my father (and who knows, for the better understanding of the Roman world?) this project never received the necessary funding – was it too transparently just a way of getting to the Soviet Union? – and might anyway have been hampered by Soviet bureaucracy and later thwarted by war. Ultimately Richard did not make his career in archaeology, though it remained a lifelong interest.

None of that is particularly remarkable. It is a course of events followed by many of those considered in this project. It is the sequel on which I should now like to focus.

It is my contention that this youthful enthusiasm for Communism, with its at that time inevitable support for the Soviet Union, far from being an illusion, or misguided or naïve, in fact helped to produce well-balanced, thoughtful citizens whose subsequent lifestyle, attitudes and values were a direct development, not a contradiction. It was an experience which cannot fail to have had a transformative effect on those involved; it must to a greater or lesser extent have changed the perspective from which they regarded the lives of those around them and shaped their future approach to the world and their practical responses to its challenges. It is this sense of an underlying continuity which makes what came afterwards relevant and illustrates a line of development that is a progression from, rather than a rejection or denial of what had gone before. It would for my parents transcend public affiliation to any one political party's ideology.

The passionate enthusiasm of youth became the pragmatism of maturity. It was an apprenticeship, something to build on and to make practical use of in the quest for a better world, one founded on firm principles of justice, fairness and equality. It would inform service to the community within the parameters of existing institutions and day-today working lives, as they endeavoured to effect some small changes to the conditions in which people lived and worked, and to suggest more effective strategies and attitudes.

While still pursuing the idea of archaeology and museum work, and after a period of working for the Refugee section of the Youth Peace Assembly (focusing on Czechoslovakia), Richard was beginning the re-orientation towards industry (mining engineering) for which he had encouragement and assistance from his father and to which he became strongly committed. Mary worked briefly in a personal assistant capacity associated with the MP, John Parker, and the Fabian Research Bureau (principally in Hornchurch), but she would ultimately never have been satisfied with a job that did not primarily consist of engaging and interacting with people. For both, this seems to have been a time (about a year) of looking around and finding their feet and waiting for the appropriate occupations to manifest themselves. War caught up with them and perhaps restricted the range of possibilities.

Going to live in Sheffield after they married was a decision made for them by the accident of job availability, but remaining there for the rest of their lives was a conscious and never regretted choice. They were peculiarly lucky in that accident. Sheffield had a distinctive character among industrial cities and one eminently suited to people with my parents' views in 1940. Traditionally radical and still predominantly working class (it has been referred to as the most proletarian city in Europe and many will remember the slogan 'Socialist Republic of South Yorkshire'), it was historically characterised by worker activism and trade unionism. Specifically, it had an active Communist element at least into the 1970s, and in 1943 my parents were still sufficiently involved with Communist affairs to have a role to play in the campaign to establish a Sheffield branch of the Society for Cultural Relations with the USSR. Sheffield was to have been the venue for the 1950 World Peace Congress to which various foreign delegates were invited, of whom only Picasso in the end received permission to enter Britain. The Congress was therefore cancelled (it was eventually held in Warsaw) but it was found necessary to convene for a single day in order to make the situation clear and Picasso duly spoke in Sheffield's City Hall. I remember talk about this and the sense of pride that Sheffield had been chosen for what was in the world of Communism and Peace a distinct honour.

Employment opportunities in Sheffield were at that time almost entirely within the steel, heavy engineering and cutlery trades, where the separation between worker and manager was frequently blurred by the nature of an accumulation of small businesses which had grown out of craftsmen's workshops, forges and small-scale specialised steel production. It was essentially a classless city, in its flourishing cultural and university-based intellectual life just as much as in its working life.

My parents were therefore able to live largely outside considerations of a class system, seeing themselves and being seen by others as individuals, not as representatives of a vested interest. They didn't have to conform, but equally there was no need to rebel. This was indeed the spirit in which my sisters and I were brought up.

For Richard more specifically, conditions were ripe for the pioneering of close cooperation between management and workforce. He believed that human beings are society's most precious resource and the policies he followed, as a much respected general manager of a firm that designed and manufactured coal-cutting and quarrying machinery, were noticed by his peers in other firms and recognised as significant. A brief preparatory spell of working underground in the coalfields of Durham, Scotland and South Wales will have given him credibility as well as experience. He always spoke warmly of the camaraderie of the pit. Given the family connection through his father's early experiences, it is conceivably not entirely accidental that Richard's field of employment was so closely involved with mining. He was in favour of nationalisation

Figure 31   Richard Clark: the end of a shift down the pit, Spennymoor,1940
(Photo: the author)

and the advances it enabled for safety and improved working conditions underground, although he was later not always in sympathy with the leaders of the NCB.

His approach to management could be seen as more than a gesture towards social levelling, but it in no way interfered with the respect he earned, equally, from his managerial colleagues throughout the mining engineering industry, and he rose to the top of both the Council for Underground Mining Machinery and the Association of British Mining Equipment Companies, culminating in his presiding as chairman over the International Mining Exhibition in Birmingham in 1977. It was through his involvement in these organisations, too, that he finally achieved his goal of a visit to the USSR – the romantic Russia of his early imaginings – for the 1967 International Mining Exhibition in Moscow, with a preliminary visit in December 1966, which I remember caused a certain amount of trepidation.

For Mary, the context in which she gave full rein to her ideals and her skills was that of helping other people to cope with the practical problems and the pressures and anxieties of their lives. She began work with the Citizens Advice Bureau, establishing with colleagues the Sheffield branch in 1940-41, where one of her roles was assisting refugees from Europe to find jobs and somewhere to live – a number of these became lifelong family friends. As was often the way for married women of her generation, she did not work full-time after I was born. She was very much a career woman but without an easily definable career and she pursued a variety of avenues in order to exploit her skills and ensure that she would never just be a housewife. She became a J.P., sitting mainly in matrimonial and juvenile courts, continuing to work with a number of voluntary organisations, including the Family Service Unit. As a Marriage Guidance counsellor from the 1950s, she rose to prominence at regional and then national level as a tutor and tutor-supervisor. This gave scope for her skills as a lecturer (begun during the war with WEA) to a range of audiences, including young people, in the North and Midlands. She later trained as a psychotherapist. She continued to put these, and many other interests and skills to work after retirement (if she can be said ever to have retired!) in U3A, UNA, and other organisations.

Both my parents had in their different ways a degree of charisma, which attracted enduring friendships and loyal associates. One of the ways in which these friendship circles developed and were consolidated was through the discussion format – dubbed the 'University of Broomhill' (the area of the city where most of them lived as young married couples) – each member of the group taking it in turns to present a paper on a topic of interest or expertise. This is an echo of the Left Book Club groups and the college-based peace groups which my mother urged when in Oxford, not to mention the discussions held within Communist cells or branches. Mary and Richard were natural choices for committees and to chair meetings – my mother was still doing that in her late 80s – and both held office in a number of local societies (e.g. the Sheffield Society for the Encouragement of Art). They were good at crystallising the heart of a discussion and framing an argument in terms that would make an appropriate contribution to decision-making.

They led useful lives, developing creatively the skills and the methodology of organisation and leadership which had been inculcated during their early political involvement – in which, of course, they were not alone. They continued to hold on to their commitment to the common good, maintaining that those who were materially, socially or educationally advantaged should strive to spread the advantages more widely. They utterly rejected the notion that private interest and personal greed, with its concomitant of callous disregard for the needs of the less fortunate, should be allowed to be the motivating criteria for the modern world. Corporate and personal greed is even now recreating the social and economic conditions which drove that generation of idealists into the arms of Communism. It was a generation which had an early encounter with a utopian world view that we would do well not to disparage.

CHAPTER NINE: PANEL DISCUSSIONS – DENIS HEALEY, PETER HENNESSY, JULIET GARDINER AND AUDIENCE CONTRIBUTIONS SUMMARISED

At all three sessions at Gresham College, in March 2013 and May 2014, there was lively discussion from the floor, and in one case there were prepared presentations from an invited Panel.

DENIS HEALEY

One of the most significant contributions was that made by (Lord) Denis Healey, at the seminar on 14th March 2013. He is one of the few survivors of that small band of 1930s enthusiasts who joined the CPGB, and we have thought it particularly relevant to include extracts from his contributions to the discussion, together with some material from his autobiography, *The Time of my Life* (1990).

In all the other individual cases covered in the course of these seminars we have to rely largely on written evidence (often quite elusive in so far as it addresses motivation) or on second-hand accounts. Denis Healey provided us with first-hand testimony on the motivations and some of the activities of those who joined the Party in the late 1930s.

Denis Healey went up to Balliol College, Oxford in October 1936. His initial interests outside his academic work were in the arts and poetry, and he devoted much time and energy to promoting interest at Oxford in modern artists. Though politics claimed more and more of his attention, he says that 'they never dominated my life at Oxford'.

And his reaction and that of his immediate friends '… was not despair. We simply worked even harder to prevent the ultimate catastrophe. So we were perhaps the most political generation in Oxford's history and our politics were overwhelmingly of the Left' (Healey 1990:33-4).

As he describes it in his autobiography, he was recruited into the CPGB by a friend, Peter Hewitt, a poet. Hewitt came from an earlier generation of student communists and had been a member of the University's October Club at a time when the Party was still highly sectarian. Now, in 1937, the communists were reaching out to a wider group and seeking to broaden its appeal by reference to the Party's role in resisting fascism. The main focus for recruitment was on Spain and the Party's martyrs, particularly John Cornford. Healey says that he found 'the element of romantic savagery' in such middle-class young communists somewhat distasteful. Nevertheless, he took the decision to join the Party, specifically because of its anti-fascist stance, as it developed in the latter part of the 1930s. As he said at the seminar,

'I joined the Communist Party when I was an undergraduate at Oxford, and for only one reason, and that was that, at that time, most of us at Oxford could see the War coming and were passionately anxious to get somebody to organise support for a war against Hitler, and the only party which was doing that at that time was the Communist Party … [We] saw the Russian communists as the only reliable anti-Hitler force, and being a member of the Labour Party did not seem enough because half the Labour Party were pacifists and the others belonged to a form of collective security which you could not define …'

As a member of the Party he pursued what he subsequently called 'the simplicities of the Popular Front', which included campaigning on behalf of the Master of his College, Balliol, in the Oxford by-election in 1938 and being elected chairman of the Labour club, having been identified by the communist faction as the most politically reliable candidate. In that capacity he helped to organise a mass meeting to protest against the introduction of conscription. In 'an atmosphere like the early days of the French Revolution' there were speeches from the local communist leader Abe Lazarus, Frank Pakenham – who had just joined the Territorial Army as a lance-corporal – and Healey himself. Though, as he subsequently reflected, he 'had made a bad mistake' and, in sum, he concludes that 'I cannot say I was proud of all my political activities in Oxford' (Healey 1990:38). Nonetheless, as he pointed out at the seminar

'... the remarkable thing really is the fact that my generation at Oxford, although very many of us were members of the Communist Party, we never wanted to do anything particularly for the Russians, whereas at Cambridge they all spied for the Russians.'

Also at the seminar he pointed out that many left the Communist Party when the Soviet Union's decision to form an alliance with the Nazis seemed to be a denial of the need to fight fascism. He himself is an example of someone who joined for a cause and departed when that cause was no longer upheld, although he did not in fact leave the Party until 1940, at the end of his last year at Oxford. Commenting on his departure at the seminar, he said:

'I was very glad because I was getting more and more fed up with the way the Communist Party was changing its policy from month to month on all sorts of central issues, without discussing it with any of its members, so that, in a sense, it was just a good thing I could move to the Labour Party.'

As he summed it up at the seminar:

'... it was a bed and breakfast Party, the Communist Party...'

And he quoted his father's dictum as putting this youthful commitment in perspective:

'When I was young and joined the Communist Party and asked my father what he thought about it, he said, "Well, if you are not a communist at the age of 20, there is something wrong with your heart; if you are still one at 30, there is something wrong with your head." And I very much appreciated that approach to the problem.'

PETER HENNESSY

Peter Hennessy began by commenting upon the remarkable trace that the thirties generation of young members of the CPGB had left on British history, although the impact was not confined to middle-class recruits – working class members also made an important contribution to a 'republic of the intellect'.

However, it was also worth remarking that although many young people were strongly affected by the climate of the times and were influenced by the left-wing discourse, as through the Left Book Club, large numbers remained in the Labour Party.

He went on to distinguish two different forms that the impact of communism had, then and later, which he called the percussive and the subversive. The percussive effect was what would in a later generation be called 'radical chic' – the appeal of something fresh at a time of greater personal freedom, as experienced in student life.

The subversive effect could be best glimpsed through the monitoring by the authorities of the activities of British communists – the surveillance, the transcripts of letters, the bugs in the Party's offices. All this stemmed from the authorities' belief that subversion was especially likely to be driven by the 'intellectual' members of the Party. The Attlee government consequently embarked after the war on a project, described by Peter Hennessy, that was designed to identify the source of danger and as far as possible neutralise it.

In closing, he stressed the importance of individual choice and circumstances in determining whether young people took the decision to join the Party.

JULIET GARDINER

Juliet Gardiner in her contribution put individual decisions to join the CPGB down to what she described as a 'political perfect storm'.

The domestic policy issues of the early thirties were the key factor in determining the choice of Party membership. However, the Party at the beginning of the thirties was still a tiny sect, and it was not until the Comintern's decision to embark on the Popular Front policy that the door opened to new middle-class recruits.

In some respects, the decision to join had similarities with religious conversions – she pointed to the fact that several members of the Day Lewis-Auden-MacNeice group had clergymen as fathers. Communism in practice could serve as a substitute for religious faith. Membership was also an all-consuming commitment – she described Philip Toynbee's experiences at Oxford, where he became the first (and only) communist President of the Oxford Union. The intensity of the engagement with the Party could effectively abolish a member's private life, as Rajani Palme Dutt, the leading Communist Party theorist, approvingly commented.

She concluded that, despite the appeal of the Party to the student generation of the later thirties, the recruits still remained a minority, if a disproportionately significant one.

COMMENTARY: OTHER ISSUES RAISED

THE 2013 SEMINARS

Points made in interventions from the floor included the need to define and differentiate between 'middle-class' and 'intellectual' CP recruits, and the presence of some of the latter on the Party's Central Committee, during the 'class against class' era.

There was also the influence of the previous generation of members (those recruited in the 1920s) on 1930s university and school students, in some cases through direct involvement in teaching them at public and grammar schools.

Comparisons were made between the limited impact of the CPGB's declared policies (revolutionary change versus engaging with Parliamentary democracy) and the Party's very significant visibility through campaigns and demonstrations. Examples of the latter included marches against unemployment and the Means Test (especially in the form of the Hunger Marches), campaigns on housing, and mass demonstrations about the impact of Nazism and the Spanish Civil War. These almost certainly had much greater impact than the 'lines' dictated by the Comintern, or even policies developed in the UK by the Party's Central Committee in King Street.

The differential attraction of the Communist Party, the Labour Party and other forms of democratic socialism and pacifism – why did some young people choose the CPGB and others not? That choice didn't necessarily mean operating in isolation. Despite the creation of specialist groups of Party members in some professions there were plenty of opportunities for Party members to work together with non-members in various professional groups, for example scientists, artists, musicians and architects, even dining clubs.

Additional reasons for choosing the CP included: the perceived impotence of the Labour Party after its crushing defeat in the 1931 General Election; the disaffiliation of the Independent Labour Party; the split within the ILP and its subsequent decline; and the CP's apparently more positive attitude towards the position of women.

The Soviet Union and Stalin – and Bolshevism were important: the effects of Soviet propaganda and visits to the USSR. There was some comment in the discussions about an apparent lack of awareness – or willed ignorance – of the famines, purges and show trials. Eventually, there was also the 1939 Nazi-Soviet Pact and its importance for individual decisions either to leave or stay in the CP.

THE 2014 SEMINAR

In the May 2014 seminar two papers were presented (reprinted in revised form above) by two historians of British communism, Professor Kevin Morgan and Geoff Andrews. There were also short presentations from six people with close family connections with thirties young communists, five of which are also now printed above.

Some contributors described personal responses by their parents or other close relatives to familiar themes, especially the need to be seen to be combating fascism, either internationally or in Britain and, above all, the paramount importance of the Spanish war.

Others underlined the distinctive character of the experience of Party membership. They stressed the commitment required of members but also some of the rewards of membership: the sense of rightness, and of being able to make sense of what was happening in the world, and of having found a safe haven; the role of the Party in encouraging self-education (not confined to working class recruits); and the mutual support found among comrades.

For some, the commitment was lifelong (cf. Philip Cohen on Len Jones); for others, some of the positive values acquired carried over into life after active Party membership (see Elizabeth Dolan's contribution on her parents).

These values included the importance of equality between comrades coming from different class, ethnic and even religious backgrounds, expressed in joint engagement in collective action to address economic and social problems.

Apart from these contributions there was also an opportunity to take part in group discussions, the points from which were reviewed with another small panel. Some issues that emerged from the group discussions might reward further attention in any future study. These included:

* The existence or non-existence of CPGB membership records as a potential source of information about recruitment in the 1930s and the obstacles to gaining access to MI5 files (especially the case of Roderick Floud's father Bernard).

* The press and radio: the attitude of the media to communism and the Party; evidence of banning CP speakers on the radio; attempts by the CP to use the media, either directly or through front organisations.

* Relationships between religion and communism, religious groups and the CPGB – individuals coming from or going to Christianity; some connections with the Quakers. Religious figures who were prepared to be spokespersons for communism, but not actually Party members, like Hewlett Johnson, the 'Red Dean'.

* Working-class attitudes to the new recruits from the middle classes. A mixed picture, depending on personal attitudes of the new middle class members (willingness to get their hands dirty) and perhaps, a degree of involvement in trade unions.

* Internationalism and anti-colonialism. General attitudes within the Party and involvement in campaigns for independence and practical help.

CHAPTER 10: REFLECTIONS

NICHOLAS DEAKIN

First, the seminars vindicated the initial assumption made by the organisers – the responses from speakers and audiences showed that it is possible to revisit this theme without the baggage of the cold war years. Nevertheless, there's a continuing need in addressing this topic to be critically alert.

So while it is still possible to see the attraction of communism for the thirties generation, in the particular circumstances of the time, and to accept that in some cases the benefits of participation may have outlasted formal Party membership, we shouldn't pass over the errors of judgment (and sometimes worse). These included unquestioning support for the USSR and deep reluctance to make any critical judgments on Soviet policies and actions. Also, the consequences of the principle of 'democratic centralism' in the Party's practices, exhibited in extreme form in the CPGB's response to the Nazi-Soviet pact. To a substantial extent, the loyalty required of Party members was blind.

Issues could also arise when the Party required involvement by its members in clandestine activity. Generally this took the form of taking office in other 'progressive' organisations without declaring one's Party membership, and then seeking to influence or control the actions of those bodies. Once the 'class against class' policy had been abandoned, these activities could in many cases be justified as an active expression of the Popular Front approach. However, espionage on behalf of the Soviet Union was an entirely different matter and we took a deliberate decision not to engage with it, although it does intrude in a couple of cases.

The motivations that led individuals to join the Party and work on its behalf were often complex. The evidence from these seminars and other sources show a variety of factors at work: in the family background, in education, in personal friendships, and through confronting the human consequences of current political, social and economic issues – the rise of fascism and the plight of the Jews, unemployment and poverty, and above all Spain.

To some extent, it may be misleading to talk about a single 'thirties generation'. Over the course of the whole decade the experiences of young adults changed as the international scene darkened and the prospect of war drew closer. The young people who demonstrated against militarism and war at the beginning of the decade were calling five years later for 'arms for Spain' and themselves enlisting in the military by the end.

But although over the decade some individual experiences were significantly different it still seems in many ways legitimate to talk about them collectively. Not least because the radical young were acutely self-aware and highly conscious of possible continuities with earlier rebel generations at different stages of recent European history and their experiences – for example, in Ireland in the first decade of the twentieth century. Roy Foster shows how young people from diverse backgrounds and initially very different beliefs coalesced, when confronted with hard questions about how independence was to be attained, into a revolutionary movement.

And then there was the supremely important example, for this group, of the Russian revolution. For them, as active members of the CPGB, the struggle to realise Lenin's initial ambitions for the Party as a 'Bolshevik' party, along the lines laid down by the Comintern, was a constant challenge. As was the task of applying the (supposed) lessons of the Soviet experience in the very different circumstances of a parliamentary democracy and working to create what the Party described in its policy documents as 'Soviet Britain'.

We can view all these questions with some detachment now, with the (priceless) benefit of hindsight. And we were fortunate, in conducting this exercise, to have been able to draw on living memories of the oldest participants as well as on family recollections. But it wouldn't have been possible without the pioneering work of those historians of communism who took the topic away from partisanship of the Party's own historians and the conspiracy theories of the cold warriors.

Finally, we hope that others will take advantage of the opportunities that exist for further research in this field, as illustrated in the many new ideas and lines for investigation that emerged during the course of the sessions at Gresham College.

AUTHOR BIOGRAPHIES

GEOFF ANDREWS

Geoff Andrews has written widely on the history of political ideas and movements. His books include *Endgames and New times; the final years of British Communism 1964–1991* (2004), *Not a normal country: Italy after Berlusconi* (2005) and *The slow food story: politics and pleasure* (2008). His new book on the life of the communist intellectual James Klugmann, *The shadow man: at the heart of the Cambridge spy circle*, is published by I B Tauris in 2015. He is Senior Lecturer in Politics at The Open University.

JANE BERNAL

Jane Bernal is currently researching a biography of her mother. Jane is a 'red nappy baby', daughter of Margot Heinemann and J D Bernal, the Marxist scientist. Until her retirement in 2013, Jane worked in the NHS as a Consultant Psychiatrist specialising in the care of people with intellectual disabilities. She was also Senior lecturer at St Georges, University of London She was a member of the COG until 1991, and was active in Marxists in Medicine and in the Medical Practitioners Union (then part of ASTMS). She is married with one son.

NORMA COHEN

Born in post-war Liverpool, Norma Cohen moved to London with her family in 1961 when her father became chief accountant at the *Morning Star*. Both parents were longstanding Communist Party members. Her mother died in 1988 before the Berlin Wall fell; her father joined the Labour Party in his late 80s. Laban movement and dance trained, she moved from teaching into performing in theatre and television. As a freelance arts/ education journalist, she wrote for *City Limits* and was Dance Editor of *TES*. Books include *Theatre Works: a guide to working in the theatre* (National Theatre/Theatre Museum) and *Bouquet with flying lovers* (Galley Cat Press). Co-founder of *Sidewalk* and *Ship of Fools* theatre companies, she currently works as a writer and actor (recently: *Who Do We Think We Are?* Visible/ Southwark Playhouse). She has written in fact, fiction and drama about her Russian/Jewish/Communist/ Liverpudlian heritage. She lives in Hackney, near her daughter Milly and grandson Sol.
Photograph by Paul Robinson

PHILIP COHEN

Philip Cohen was born in Liverpool in 1949 and lived there until he was 12 when his family moved to London. He has been a journalist, writer and PR professional, and worked for the London 2012 Olympics. His parents Eve and Eric Cohen, as well as uncle Len Jones, were long-time CPGB members and as a child he was taken on demonstrations and marches against the bomb, the Vietnam War and apartheid. This early experience motivated him to put together a book, *Children of the Revolution* (Lawrence and Wishart, 1997). He is in the second year of studying for a PhD on nuclear weapons and propaganda 1957-63.

NICHOLAS DEAKIN

Nicholas Deakin read Modern History at Oxford University and took a doctorate at the University of Sussex. He has worked as a civil servant and in local government. He has also chaired national and local voluntary bodies. From 1980 to 1998 he was Professor of Social Policy and Administration at the University of Birmingham and was subsequently a visiting professor at the University of Warwick and then at the London School of Economics. In 1995-6 he chaired the Independent Commission on the Future of the Voluntary Sector in England. He was Vice-Chair of the Baring Foundation, and a member of the Foundation's Independence Panel. He has published many books and articles on different aspects of social policy.

ELIZABETH DOLAN

The eldest of three sisters, Elizabeth Dolan was born in Sheffield in 1945. Her parents belonged to the 1930s generation of undergraduate Communists. After a degree in French at St. Hugh's College, Oxford, she trained as a nursery and infant teacher, working with under-fives in maintained primary schools in London and Essex. She joined the National Union of Teachers as a student, was for several years a local branch secretary and remains active as a retired member. Married, with two children and six grandchildren, her professional involvement in early-years education has happily interacted with family life and her continuing interest in literature.

RODERICK FLOUD

Roderick Floud was Provost of Gresham College from 2008-2014. An economic historian, he taught at London, Cambridge and Stanford Universities and was vice-chancellor of London Metropolitan University, President of Universities UK and Vice-President of the European University Association. He is the editor of the major textbook on modern British economic history and author of books on the history of human heights and weights; he is currently writing an economic history of British gardening. He is a Fellow of the British Academy, of the Academy of the Social Sciences and of the Academia European and was knighted for services to higher education.

HAMISH MACGIBBON

Hamish MacGibbon was born in 1936 in the month when the Spanish Civil War started and his parents joined the Party. Educated at various progressive schools during World War Two, he went to Westminster School followed by National Service, a degree in history at Cambridge, and a start in publishing at Heinemann. After 25 years in that firm he founded his own publishing company which he ran for the next two decades. Like his parents, he took part in the first Aldermaston March and subsequent ones. A member of the Labour Party (just) for sixty years, he was a councillor for the Labour Camden Council in the late 1960s.

KEVIN MORGAN

Kevin Morgan is Professor of Politics and Contemporary History at the University of Manchester and an editor of the journal Twentieth Century Communism. He has published widely on communism and the British labour movement including studies of Harry Pollitt, Ramsay MacDonald and the Webbs. His latest book is *Bolshevism, syndicalism and the general strike: The lost internationalist world of A. A. Purcell* (2013). His next, to be published in 2015, will be a study of communism and the cult of the individual.

GLOSSARY

AIA: Artists' International Association

BUF: British Union of Fascists

Comintern: Communist International

CPGB: Communist Party of Great Britain

CUSS: Cambridge University Socialist Society

FSS: Federation of Student Societies

GRU: Glavnoye razvedyvatel'noye upravleniye (Soviet Army Intelligence)

IB: International Brigade

ILP: Independent Labour Party

ILS: International Lenin School

LBC: Left Book Club

LLY: Labour League of Youth

LNU: League of Nations Union

LRD: Labour Research Department

NKVD: Narodnyy Komissariat Vnutrennikh Del (The People's Commissariat for Internal Affairs)

NUS: National Union of Students

NUWM: National Unemployed Workers Movement

OULC: Oxford University Labour Club

POUM: Partido Obrero de Unificación Marxista

PPU: Peace Pledge Union

RAMC: Royal Army Medical Corps

RME: Rassemblement Mondial des Etudiants (World Student Association Against War and Fascism)

U3A: University of the Third Age

ULF: University Labour Federation

UNA: United Nations Association

USSR: Union of Soviet Socialist Republics

VOKS: All-Union Society for Cultural Relations with Foreign Countries

WEA: Workers' Education Association

YCL: Young Communist League

BIBLIOGRAPHY

Andrew, Christopher. (2009) *The Defence of the Realm: the authorised history of MI5*. London: Allen Lane.

Andrews, Geoff, Fishman, Nina and Morgan, Kevin. (1995) *Opening the Books*. London: Pluto Press.

Andrews, Geoff. (2015) *James Klugmann, the shadow man: at the heart of the Cambridge spy circle*. London: I B Tauris

Anon. (1932) *Those in Authority*. D.A. Hedley (King's), President of the A.D.C.. *Granta*, November 4th 1932:63.

Barrett-Brown, Michael. (2005) *From Tito to Milosevic*. London: Merlin Press.

Bounds, Philip. (2012) *British Communism and the politics of literature 1928-1938*. London: Merlin Press.

Boyle, Andrew. (1979) *The climate of treason*. London: Hutchinson.

Brandon, Piers. (2000) *The dark valley: a panorama of the 1930s*. London: Jonathan Cape.

Branson, Noreen. (1985) *History of the CPGB 1927-41*. London: Lawrence and Wishart.

Branson, Noreen and Heinemann, Margot. (1971) *Britain in the Thirties*. London: Weidenfeld and Nicolson.

Brecht, Bertold. (1979) *Poems 1913-1956*. London: Eyre Methuen.

Brendon, Piers. (2000) *The Dark Valley: a panorama of the 1930s*. London: Jonathan Cape.

Brinson, Charmian and Dove, Richard. (2014) *A Matter of Intelligence: MI5 and the surveillance of anti-Nazi Refugees 1933-50*. Manchester: Manchester UP.

Broda, Paul. (2011) *Scientist Spies: A memoir of my three parents and the Atom Bomb*. Kibworth: Matador.

Brown, Alec. (1936) *The Fate of the Middle Classes.* London: Gollancz

Brown, Andrew. (2005) *J.D.Bernal, the sage of Science.* Oxford: OUP

Brown, Archie. (2009) *The Rise and Fall of Communism.* London: Bodley Head

Buchanan, Tom. (1991) *The Spanish Civil War and the British Labour Movement.* Cambridge: CUP.

Butler, John. (2011) *The Red Dean of Canterbury: the public and private faces of Hewlett Johnson.* London: Scala.

Carter, Miranda. (2002) *Anthony Blunt: his lives.* London: Pan.

Ceadel, Martin. (2010) *Semi-detached Idealists: The British Peace Movement and International Relations 1854-1945.* Oxford: OUP.

Cecil, Robert. (1988) *A Divided Life: a biography of Donald Maclean.* London: Bodley Head.

Clark, Jon, Heinemann, Margot, Margolies, David and Smee, Carole. (1979) *Culture and Crisis in Britain in the 1930s.* London: Lawrence and Wishart.

Cohen, Phillip. (1979) *Children of the Revolution.* London: Lawrence and Wishart

Collison, Peter. (1963) *The Cutteslowe Walls: a study in social class.* London: Faber and Faber.

Communist Party of Great Britain. (1937) *It can be done: Report of the Fourteenth Congress.* London: CPGB

Communist Party of Great Britain. (1938) *For Peace and Plenty: Report of the Fifteenth Congress.* London: CPGB.

Conradi, Peter. (2001) *Iris Murdoch: a life.* London: Harper Collins.

Conradi, Peter. (2001) *A Very English hero: the making of Frank Thompson.* London: Bloomsbury.

Croft, Andy (ed)(1998) *A Weapon in the Struggle: The cultural history of the Communist Party in Britain.* London: Pluto Press.

Croft, Andy. (2001) 'The Young Men are Moving Together: the case of Randall Swingler' in McIlroy, Morgan and Campbell, *Party People, Communist Lives*. London: Lawrence and Wishart.

Cunningham, Valentine. (1989) *British writers of the Thirties*. Oxford: OUP

Day Lewis, Cecil. (1960) *The Buried Day*. London: Chatto and Windus.

Day Lewis, Cecil. (1937) *The Mind in Chains*. London: Frederick Muller.

Ferns, Henry. (1938) *Reading from left to right: one man's political history*. Toronto: University of Toronto Press

Ferry, Georgina. (1998) *Dorothy Hodgkin: a life*. London: Granta Books

Forbes, Duncan (ed) (2013). *Edith Tudor-Hart: in the shadow of tyranny*. Edinburgh: National Galleries of Scotland and Wien Museum.

Gardiner, Juliet. (2010) *The Thirties: An intimate history*. London: Harper Press.

Green, John. (2014), *Britain's Communists: the untold story*. London: Artery Publications.

Greene, Graham (ed)(1934) *W.H.Auden: 'Honour: Gresham's School, Holt'*. *The Old School*. London: Jonathan Cape.

Haden Guest, Carmel. (1939) *David Guest: a scientist fights for freedom, 1911-1938*. London: Lawrence and Wishart.

Harrison, Brian. (1991) 'Oxford and the Labour Movement', *Twentieth Century British History, Vol 2*, No 3:226-271.

Hart, Jenifer. (1998). *Ask me No More*. London: Peter Halban.

Healey, Denis. (1990) *The Time of my Life*. London: Penguin.

Heinemann, Margot. (1933) 'On the Ethics of Demonstrations: A Dialogue between Peace-Lovers.' *Thersites*, no. 102:4-6.

Hobsbawm, Eric. (2002) *Interesting Times: a twentieth century life*. London: ALPP.

Hobsbawm, Eric. (2007) 'Cadres: Communism in Britain', review article in *London Review of Books*. vol 29 no 8 26 April.

Howarth, T.E.B. (1978) *Cambridge between Two Wars.* London: Collins.

Hyde, Douglas. (1953) *I Believed.* London: Pan Books.

Isherwood, Christopher. (1946) *Prater Violet.* London: Methuen.

Jacobs, Joe. (1991) *Out of the Ghetto.* London: Phoenix.

Jones, Leonard Abraham. (1998) *Pages from the Life of a Teacher.* Halle an der Saale.

Jones, Mervyn. (1987) *Chances: an autobiography.* London: Verso.

Kiernan, V. G. (1989) 'Herbert Norman's Cambridge '. In *Poets, Politics and the People.* London: Verso

Kiernan, Victor et al (Roger Simon, George Barnard, Ralph Russell, John Maynard Smith, Cyril Claydon, Norman Lindop, Dorothy Wedderburn, Peter Worsley, Dorothy Thompson, June Bean). (c. 2004) 'Cambridge Communism in the 1930s and 1940s: a collection of Cambridge recollections'. *Socialist History*, 24: 39-59

Klingender, F. D. (1935) *The Condition of Clerical Labour in Britain.* London: Martin Lawrence

Klugmann, James. (1979) 'The Crisis in the Thirties: a view from the Left' in Jon Clark et al: *Culture and Crisis in Britain in the 30s.* London: Lawrence and Wishart.

Knox, Bernard. (1989) *Essays : Ancient and Modern.* Baltimore: Johns Hopkins University Press.

Knox, Bernard. (1998) *Premature Anti-Fascist.* (University of Illinois, http://www.english.uiuc.edu/maps/scw/knox.htm. The Abraham Lincoln Brigade Archives – Bill Susman Lecture Series. King Juan Carlos I of Spain Center – New York University)

Kushner, Tony. (2000) *Remembering Cable Street.* Elstree: Valentine Mitchell.

Laity, Paul (ed)(2001) *Left Book Club anthology.* London: Gollancz.

Laybourne, Keith and Murphy, Dylan. (1999) *Under the Red Flag: a history of communism in Britain.* London: Alan Sutton.

Leader, Zachary. (2006) *The Life of Kingsley Amis*. London: Jonathan Cape.

Left Book Club publications (1936-) seriatim.

Lehmann, John, Jackson, T.A. and Day Lewis, Cecil. (1937) *Ralph Fox: a writer in arms*. London: Lawrence and Wishart.

Lessing, Doris. (1995) *Under My Skin*. London: Flamingo.

Linehan, Thomas. (2007) *Communism in Britain 1920-1939*. Manchester: Manchester UP.

McCarthy, Helen. (2011) *The British People and the League of Nations 1918-45*. Manchester: Manchester UP.

MacEwen, Malcolm. (1991) *The Greening of a Red*. London: Pluto Press.

MacGibbon, Jean. (1984) *I meant to marry him: a personal memoir*. London: Victor Gollancz.

McIntosh, Ronald. (2014) *Turbulent Times*. London: Biteback.

McIlroy, John, Morgan, Kevin and Campbell, Alan (eds)(2001) *Party people, Communist lives – explorations in biography*. London: Lawrence and Wishart.

Macleod, Alison. (1997) *The Death of Uncle Joe*. London: Merlin Press.

MacNeice, Louis. (1939) *Autumn Journal*. London: Faber.

Madge, Charles. (1986) *Britain by Mass Observation*. London: Cresset Press.

Mayhew, Christopher. (1987) *Time to Explain*. London: Hutchinson.

Makarenko, A.S. (1955) *The Road to Life: An Epic of Education*. Moscow: Foreign Languages Publishing House.

Miller, Karl. (2012) *Eric Hobsbawm*, London Review of Books, 25.10.12:12

Mirsky, Dmitri (tr. Brown, Alec). (1935) *The Intelligentsia of Great Britain*. London: Victor Gollancz

Morgan, Kevin. (1989) *Against fascism and war: ruptures and continuities in British Communist policy 1935-41*. Manchester: Manchester UP.

Morgan, Kevin. (2006) *Bolshevism and the British Left. Part One: Labour Legends and Russian Gold.* London: Lawrence and Wishart.

Morgan, Kevin, Cohen, Gidon and Flinn, Andrew. (2007) *Communists and British Society 1920-1991.* London: Rivers Oram.

Morgan, Kevin. (2011) Socialists and mobility in twentieth-century Britain: images and experiences in the life-histories of British communists, *Social History*, 36:2.

Morgan, Kevin. (1993) *Harry Pollitt.* Manchester: Manchester UP.

Newton, Kenneth. (1969) *The Sociology of British Communism.* London: ALPP.

Orwell, George. (1937) *The Road to Wigan Pier.* London: Victor Gollancz.

Orwell, George. (1940) *Selected essays, esp. Inside the Whale.* London: Victor Gollancz.

Pascal, Roy. (1934) *The Nazi dictatorship.* London: Routledge.

Paul, Alwin. (1933) Achievements of National Socialism, what the NS government has hitherto achieved. *Granta*, Christmas issue.

Pimlott, Ben. (1993) Two men who Saw Red (Harry Pollitt and Rajani Palme Dutt), review article in *The Independent* 15.8.

Pollitt, Harry. (1937) *Speech to Left Book Club meeting, Albert Hall 7.2.37.* Manchester: CPGB Archive.

Pollitt, Harry. (1940) *Serving my Time.* London: Lawrence and Wishart.

Preston, Paul. (2006) *The Spanish Civil War: reaction, revolution and revenge.* London: Harper Perennial.

Raine, Kathleen. (1975) *The Land Unknown.* London: Hamish Hamilton.

Rattenbury, Arnold. (2001) 'The Bad Old Civilisation', *London Review of Books* 23:19. 4 October.

Reynolds, David. (2013) *The Long Shadow.* London: Simon and Schuster.

Roberts, Michael (ed). (1933) *New Country.* London: Hogarth Press.

Rosenberg, David. (2001) *Battle for the East End.* Nottingham: Five Leaves Publications.

Russell, Ralph. (2001) *Findings, Keepings: life, communism and everything.* London: Shola Books.

Samuel, Raphael. (2006) *The Lost World of British Communism.* London: Verso.

Saville, John. (2003) *Memoirs from the Left.* London: Merlin Press.

Sloan, Pat (ed). (1938) *John Cornford: a memoir.* London: Jonathan Cape.

Smith, D.S. (2012) *D.S.Mirsky, a Russian-English Life.* Oxford: OUP.

Smith, Stephen A. (2014) *The Oxford Handbook of the History of Communism.* Oxford: OUP.

Spender, Stephen. (1978) *The Thirties and after.* London: Macmillan.

Stansky, Peter and Abrahams, William. (1966) *Journey to a Frontier: Julian Bell and John Cornford: their lives and the 1930s.* London: Constable.

Steiner, Zara. (2010) *The Triumph of the Dark: European International history 1933-39.* Oxford: OUP.

Strachey, John. (1938) *Why You should be a Socialist.* London: Victor Gollancz.

Taylor, Elizabeth. (1945) *At Mrs Lippincote's.* London: Peter Davies.

Thomas, Hugh. (1973) *John Strachey.* London: Eyre Methuen.

Thompson, Dorothy. (1993) 'The Personal and the Political', *New Left Review,* 200:87-100.

Thompson, E.P. (1978) Outside the whale *(1960), The poverty of theory and other essays.* London: Merlin.

Thompson, Willie. (1992) *The Good Old Cause.* London: Pluto Press.

Thorpe, Andrew. (2000) *The British Communist Party and Moscow 1920-43.* Manchester: Manchester UP.

Toynbee, Philip. (1954) *Friends Apart.* London: MacGibbon and Kee.

Trevelyan, Julian. (1957) *Indigo Days.* London: MacGibbon and Kee.

Upward, Edward. (1962) *In the Thirties*. London: Heinemann.

Watson, Don. (2014) *No Justice without a Struggle: The National Unemployed Workers' Movement in the North East of England 1920-1940*. London: Merlin.

Werskey, Gary. (1978) *The Visible College*. London: Allen Lane.

West, Alick. (1969) *One man in his time*. London: George Allen and Unwin.

Williams-Ellis, Amabel. (1988) *All Stracheys are cousins*. London: Weidenfeld and Nicolson.

Wood, Neal. (1959) *Communism and British Intellectuals*. London: Victor Gollancz.

Wright, Peter. (1987) *Spycatcher: the candid autobiography of a senior intelligence officer*. London: Viking Penguin.

Biographical material

Jack Gaster (in family papers)

Charles Madge (at University of Sussex Library)

Margot Kettle (in collection at People's History Library, Manchester)

Security Service Files

Jack Gaster (KV2/1558/9)

Margot Heinemann (KV2/2527)

Thomas Hodgkin (KV2/3680)

Malcolm MacEwen (KV2/2985)

Frank Meyer (KV2/3501)

Graeme Shankland (KV2/3109)

Douglas Springhall (KV2/1596)

George Thomson (KV2/1842)

Personal Papers
Clark family
Gaster /Lynd family
Margot Heinemann
François Lafitte
Charles Madge

Archives
Birmingham University
CPGB collection in People's History Museum, Manchester
Sussex University
Westminster School

INDEX

Lewis, David 29
Lindsay, Alexander (Sandy) 44
Lynd, Maire 26, 43, 48, 65

M

MacGibbon, James 3, 5, 132, 133, 137
Maclean, Donald 21, 27, 91, 95, 174
MacNeice, Louis 40
Madge, Charles 26, 53, 55, 65, 180, 181
Makarenko, Anton 118, 120, 177
Marx House 77
Mass Observation 4, 53, 57, 177
McEachran, Frank 93
McGree, Leon 125
McIntosh, Mary 3, 5, 8, 65, 139, 140, 146
McIntosh, Ronald (Ronnie) 13, 139
Means Test 19, 20, 112, 161
Meyer, Frank Strauss 29, 35, 62, 98, 180
MI5 12, 13, 48, 62, 66, 102, 163, 173
Miller, Karl 15
Mirsky, Prince Dmitri 27, 28, 29, 55, 177, 179

Mosley, Oswald 29, 32, 35, 48, 49, 108, 113, 116, 118, 125, 148
Murdoch, Iris 26

N

National Cultural Committee 78
National Unemployed Workers Movement (NUWM) 32
National Union of Students (NUS) 72, 82, 172
Nazi-Soviet Pact 71, 87, 162
Nirenstein, Minna 88
NKVD (The People's Commisariat for Internal Affairs) 135, 172

O

October Club 29, 30, 96, 98, 157
Orwell, George 46, 53
Owen, Wilfred 18
Oxford 13, 27, 29, 30, 34, 35, 37, 39, 44, 45, 71, 72, 76, 79, 96, 110, 142, 145, 148, 154, 156, 157, 158, 160, 169, 170, 172, 175, 179
Oxford University Labour Club (OULC) 34, 45, 148, 172

P

Pacifism 90, 94, 108, 143, 161
Pakenham, Frank 158
Parker, John 150
Parsons, Steve 77
Paul, Alwin 108
Peace Ballot 29, 34
Peace Pledge Union 29, 35, 172
People's History Museum 25, 33, 66, 181
Picasso, Pablo 151
Pincher, Chapman 12
Pollitt, Harry 24, 25, 43, 47, 56, 64, 69, 71, 80, 116, 128, 171, 178
Popular Front 35, 36, 44, 45, 71, 76, 77, 78, 81, 85, 100, 102, 104, 113, 135, 157, 160, 164
POUM (Partido Obrero de Unificación Marxista) 56

Q

Quakers 163

R

Reichstag fire 32, 77

RME (Rassemblement Mondiale des Etudiants) 101, 102, 104, 172
Roberts, Michael 53
Roedean School 109
Rosenheim, Anna Browne 88
Rosenheim, Charles 91
Rycroft, Charles 100

S

Saklatvala, Shapurgi 116
Samuel, Raphael 42, 88
Saville, John 16, 70
Shaw, George Bernard 75
Sheppard, Dick 35
Simon, Brian 91, 100
Simon, Ernest 80, 91
Simon, Roger 80, 86, 176
Socialist League, The 75
South Hampstead High School, London 90, 109, 141
Spain 10, 25, 35, 36, 40, 41, 43, 45, 48, 56, 62, 63, 69, 70, 72, 78, 80, 83, 98, 102, 125, 132, 134, 143, 157, 165, 176
Spanish Civil War 127, 128, 161, 174, 178
Spender, Stephen 53
Stalin, Josef 15, 16, 47, 55, 70, 75, 81, 83, 116, 120, 162

Stebbing, Susan 89
St Leonard's Girls' School 132
Strachey, John 53, 179
Swingler, Randall 24, 175

T

Thompson, Frank 26, 45, 174
Thomson, Alexander Raven 118
Toller, Ernst 116
Toynbee, Philip 43, 72, 160
Trinity College, Cambridge 96, 98
Trinity Hall, Cambridge 96
Trotsky/Trotskyists 63, 125

U

Uffpuff (United Front of Popular Forces) 24
Unemployment 10, 19, 20, 32, 79, 116, 134, 142, 161, 165
Unity Theatre 77
University Labour Federation (ULF) 35, 78, 172
Upward, Edward 46, 53
USSR 27, 32, 36, 44, 46, 61, 63, 71, 72, 73, 74, 83, 136, 150, 153, 162, 164, 172

V

Verney, Tessa 148

W

Webb, Sidney / Beatrice 74
West, Alick 85
Westminster School 22, 23, 27, 66
Wheeler, Mortimer 148
Winchester College 26
Workers' Education Association (WEA) 154, 172
World Peace Congress 150

Y

Young Communist League (YCL) 124, 128, 172

Risograph printed on Munken Lynx 300 gsm (Cover) and Evercopy 80gsm.
The fonts that were used in this book are Adobe Caslon Pro and Halis R.